Introduction

The Decline of Common Sense

Practical wisdom, once the foundation of decision-making and business expertise, seems to be diminishing in today's corporate landscape. It was previously a crucial factor for success—a blend of practical knowledge, intuition, and logical reasoning that enabled businesses to grow steadily, solve problems effectively, and navigate obstacles with ease. However, as the business landscape has transformed, the approach to decision-making has often shifted, frequently at the cost of this once-prized attribute.

In the past, common sense was about trusting experience, applying fundamental principles, and making logical decisions based on the realities of a situation. It involved understanding human behavior, learning from the past, and taking direct, practical actions to move the business forward. Whether it was negotiating deals, managing teams, or addressing customer concerns, the best leaders had an innate ability to cut through the clutter and focus on what truly mattered. This common-sense approach led to decisions that were not only intelligent but also actionable and aligned with the company's long-term objectives.

However, the modern corporate landscape has become increasingly complex. The explosion of digital information, together with the growing sophistication of business models, has eroded the simplicity that common sense once provided. Instead of relying on basic principles, many leaders today are overwhelmed by the sheer volume of data and trends that demand their attention. This overload of information, while theoretically useful, often obscures the straightforward solutions that common sense would otherwise bring to light. Today, many business leaders find themselves relying on overly complicated processes—drowning in data, lost in intricate financial models, and succumbing to industry trends that seem important but ultimately distract from core objectives. The straightforward thinking that once defined good leadership is now clouded by a never-ending chase for the perfect, data-driven answer.

The Shift Away from Practicality

The shift towards data-driven decision making has several underlying factors. The proliferation of big data and sophisticated analytics tools has provided businesses with unprecedented access to information, enabling insights that were previously unimaginable. While data undoubtedly holds immense value, an over-reliance on it has led to a phenomenon known as "analysis paralysis." Leaders often feel compelled to scrutinize every possible metric before deciding, sifting through countless data points, reports, and forecasts. In doing so, they lose sight of the obvious, practical solutions that common sense would naturally suggest. In many cases, business leaders become so engrossed in searching for the perfect answer within the data that they fail to recognize the clear path right in front of them.

This trend is worsened by the increasing complexity of business models. Contemporary organizations are expansive, with multiple divisions, functions, and specializations. While specialization can cultivate expertise, it can also create silos—isolated departments narrowly focused on their areas of knowledge without considering the bigger picture. The result is that simple, common-sense decisions become buried beneath layers of specialized jargon, technical processes, and approval chains. A basic decision that could have been made in a matter of hours may now take days, if not weeks, to navigate the intricacies of modern corporate hierarchies.

Furthermore, the tendency to overcomplicate the decision-making process is frequently motivated by a fear of committing errors. Today's leaders are held to increasingly stringent standards of accountability, with their every action being meticulously measured and monitored. This environment cultivates a risk-averse culture where decision-makers feel compelled to engage in excessive analysis, double-checking, and the involvement of multiple layers of approval, all to protect against potential mistakes. However, this cautious approach often results in missed opportunities, as practical and straightforward solutions are overshadowed by the perceived necessity for perfection.

The Impact of Rapid Innovation

The digital era has brought about a time of swift innovation and continuous disruption. While the ability to adapt and innovate is essential for remaining competitive, the pressure to constantly chase emerging trends can leave businesses feeling directionless. Many organizations find themselves hastily adopting new technologies, industry buzzwords, and strategic approaches without fully considering whether they align with the company's core values or address practical business needs. For instance, businesses may rush to implement artificial intelligence or blockchain solely because they are trending topics, rather than because they provide a clear advantage to their operations. Consequently, companies sacrifice long-term stability in pursuit of short-lived fads, abandoning the prudent practice of aligning every decision with the broader organizational objectives.

This pressure to continuously innovate frequently results in what is referred to as "shiny object syndrome"—the propensity for businesses to pursue novel, attention-grabbing solutions while overlooking the fundamental, time-tested principles that have long underpinned their success. Rather than evaluating new trends through a lens of practical reasoning, organizations become captivated by the thrill of being at the forefront, often adopting technology or strategies that unnecessarily complicate their operations without addressing core issues.

The digital era has transformed the decision-making process, with real-time access to global data and rapidly evolving markets compressing timelines. Leaders now face mounting pressure to react swiftly to changes, often leading to hurried choices based on partial information or impulsive responses to market fluctuations. In this fast-moving landscape, the thoughtful, level-headed approach that practical wisdom demands is frequently abandoned in favor of hasty actions and superficial remedies.

The Consequences of Complexity

The prevalence of complex, overcomplicated solutions has made it increasingly challenging to find practical, common-sense approaches to business leadership and strategy. Many organizations have become overly reliant on intricate, engineered solutions that often miss the mark, failing to deliver the intended results. The overcomplication of processes, the chase for the latest trends, and the overwhelming influx of data have left numerous businesses vulnerable to inefficiency, poor decision-making, and ultimately, failure.

We can see real-world examples of businesses that have lost sight of common-sense principles. Some companies have pursued overly ambitious digital transformation projects, promising to revolutionize their operations, but instead, these initiatives have collapsed under the weight of their own complexity. Others have followed management fads that sounded revolutionary but proved impractical to implement, leaving the organization in a worse position than before. These failures underscore the dangers of abandoning practical, experience-based decision-making in favor of convoluted, theoretical approaches.

The core of this issue is a fundamental misunderstanding: more information does not necessarily lead to better decisions. In fact, in many cases, it leads to worse decisions because it obscures the most obvious and sensible path forward. Common sense, with its emphasis on simplicity, clarity, and practicality, offers a vital counterbalance to this trend. By relying on experience, applying basic principles, and making logical decisions based on the realities of a situation, businesses can avoid many of the pitfalls associated with overcomplication.

In summary, the decline of common sense is not a minor issue - it represents a profound shift that has left many businesses struggling to maintain efficiency, agility, and focus. The key to future business success lies not in pursuing complexity, but in rediscovering the simple, practical wisdom that has always been at the heart of effective leadership and sound strategy.

Why It Matters Now More Than Ever

The diminishing presence of practical reasoning in the business world is not merely a gentle transition—it carries substantial and wide-ranging implications for contemporary organizations. In a period defined by intensified market competition, ceaseless innovation, and perpetual change, the lack of practical wisdom can become a critical vulnerability. Without common sense, businesses risk compromising their agility, clarity, and capacity for sound decision-making. In an environment where swift, well-informed action is crucial, the erosion of this once-essential characteristic can spell disaster for leadership, employee productivity, and the long-term success of the organization.

Leadership Effectiveness

For leaders, the absence of common sense creates a dangerous gap between their intentions and the actual execution of their plans. Leaders who overcomplicate their decision-making processes, often by excessively analyzing data or adhering to rigid frameworks, struggle to provide the clear, decisive direction that their teams need to succeed. When decisions become mired in complexity, leaders can find themselves paralyzed by indecision, unable to provide the quick, confident guidance that keeps a company progressing forward. This hesitation or confusion then trickles down to their teams, leading to misaligned objectives, disjointed strategies, and a lack of clear priorities.

In contrast, leaders who rely on common sense are able to cut through the noise and complexity. They trust their instincts when necessary, balance analysis with intuition, and make decisions that are grounded in practicality and the real needs of the business. These leaders are able to simplify complex problems, avoid unnecessary bureaucracy, and empower their teams to act decisively. Their leadership style fosters an environment of clarity and focus, where goals are straightforward, roles are clear, and teams are aligned around a shared mission.

The implications of not employing common sense in leadership extend beyond individual decision-making. It affects the overall culture of the organization. A lack of clarity at the top leads to poor communication throughout the company, as managers struggle to interpret and implement the overly complex directives coming from above. When leaders fail to demonstrate practical wisdom, they inadvertently create a culture of confusion, where employees are unsure of their roles, priorities become muddled, and the organization lacks the agility to respond to challenges effectively.

Employee Productivity and Engagement

The absence of common sense in leadership can be highly damaging for employees. It manifests in various challenges that hinder productivity, creativity, and morale. Overly complicated procedures, indecisive leadership, and excessive bureaucracy make it difficult for employees to perform their jobs efficiently. When leaders burden employees with unnecessary rules, processes, or approval chains, they create an environment that stifles practical, results-oriented thinking. Employees end up wasting valuable time navigating cumbersome processes that could be simplified through common-sense approaches.

Over time, this type of work environment leads to frustration, disengagement, and low morale. Employees are stripped of their autonomy and creativity, forced to operate within rigid structures that limit their ability to think critically or use their own judgment. Instead of being empowered to solve problems and make decisions, they feel like mere cogs in a machine, with no sense of ownership over their work. This not only reduces overall productivity, but also diminishes the innovative spirit that drives organizations forward.

Reintroducing common sense into the workplace means giving employees the freedom to think for themselves. It involves removing unnecessary rules, simplifying procedures, and encouraging employees to use their judgment to make decisions based on the situation at hand. This empowerment boosts productivity and creativity, as employees feel more engaged and invested in their work. They become problem-solvers rather than mere process-followers, and the entire organization benefits from a more dynamic and effective workforce.

Moreover, a common-sense approach fosters a culture of trust and accountability. When employees are trusted to make decisions based on practical considerations, they take greater ownership of their roles. They are more likely to innovate, take initiative, and contribute to the company's success because they feel their contributions are valued and their judgment is respected.

Long-Term Organizational Success

At the organizational level, the lack of common sense poses a serious threat to long-term success. Companies that prioritize complexity over clarity find themselves less agile, slower to adapt, and more vulnerable to disruption. In fast-paced markets where trends and customer needs evolve rapidly, businesses that fail to streamline their decision-making or ignore practical, simple solutions risk falling behind.

When common sense is absent, organizations become weighed down by unnecessary layers of decision-making and over-engineered solutions that often miss the mark. Instead of moving swiftly to capitalize on opportunities or address challenges, they get bogged down in excessive analysis, unnecessary meetings, and convoluted processes.

This creates a significant disadvantage in competitive markets where the ability to act quickly and decisively is often key to survival.

Furthermore, the over-reliance on complex, theoretical approaches - whether intricate financial models, trend-chasing strategies, or rigid management frameworks - can cause businesses to lose sight of the core values and principles that drive sustainable growth. Common sense, with its emphasis on practicality, simplicity, and adaptability, is essential for building a resilient, stable organization. It ensures that decisions are aligned with the company's long-term goals, not just short-term trends, or immediate pressures.

In times of crisis or market shifts, businesses grounded in common sense are more likely to weather the storm. They rely on clear, practical decision-making, focusing on what truly matters and avoiding the distractions of overcomplicated solutions. These businesses are not easily swayed by fads or overwhelmed by complexity; instead, they stick to sound, experience-based judgment that guides them through uncertainty with confidence and clarity.

Common Sense as a Competitive Advantage

In the current business climate, where change is the only constant, the ability to make swift and practical decisions is more crucial than ever before. The rapid pace of technological advancements, shifting market demands, and global economic pressures require businesses to be adaptable, decisive, and focused. In this environment, common sense provides a vital competitive edge. It allows businesses to stay grounded, prioritize what matters most, and navigate complexity with clarity and purpose.

The beauty of common sense lies in its simplicity. It cuts through the noise of over-complication, bringing clarity to decision-making and ensuring that organizations remain agile and responsive to change. Companies that embrace common sense are able to focus on their strengths, eliminate unnecessary distractions, and make decisions that align with their long-term goals. This positions them to innovate, adapt, and thrive in the fast-paced business world.

Reintroducing common sense into the business world is not just about simplifying processes or making quicker decisions; it's about restoring balance. It's about empowering people to use their judgment, trust their instincts, and make decisions that are both practical and effective. It's about building organizations that are not only efficient and productive but also resilient and capable of thriving in the face of change.

The Path Forward

This book will examine how common sense can be revived and leveraged as a powerful tool for leadership, decision-making, and organizational success. By stripping away the unnecessary and returning to the fundamentals of sound judgment, businesses can establish a foundation for sustained growth and success in the modern world. From empowering employees and cultivating a culture of trust to simplifying decision-making processes and staying grounded in core values, common sense provides a clear path to long-term success in a complex, fast-paced business environment.

Chapter 1: Defining Common Sense in Business

This chapter establishes the groundwork for the entire book by examining the true meaning of common sense in a business environment. It's not merely about instinct or apparent solutions - in the business world, common sense refers to a blend of practical wisdom, judgment based on experience, and straightforward decision-making. By defining and contextualizing this term, we can better understand why its decline has had such a profound impact on leadership, employee engagement, and organizational success. Through this chapter, readers will develop a clear understanding of how to apply common sense effectively in a contemporary business setting.

What Is Common Sense in Business?

In the business world, common sense refers to practical, experience-based thinking that emphasizes straightforward, logical solutions to challenges. While this concept may seem intuitive or obvious, it is often overlooked in favor of more complex, theoretical approaches, especially as businesses grow larger and face more sophisticated problems. However, this practical wisdom is essential for business leaders to stay grounded and focused on what truly matters, despite the overwhelming pressures of innovation, data overload, and rapid change.

Common sense in business manifests itself in several keyways that are crucial for leadership, decision-making, and overall company culture. This practical, down-to-earth approach serves as a powerful, yet often underutilized, asset in the corporate world.

Practicality Over Complexity

The foundation of common sense lies in practical thinking, focusing on what actually works, rather than getting bogged down in unnecessary complexity. The most straightforward solution is often the best one, and common sense is about identifying those simple, effective solutions that cut through confusion and over-analysis.

For instance, consider a company facing declining sales. A leader driven by complex, theoretical approaches might propose an elaborate multi-stage restructuring, expensive branding overhauls, or adopting new technology platforms to boost visibility. While these strategies may have merit, they often overlook the most basic solutions—listening to customer feedback and improving the product or service itself. A common-sense approach would focus on the fundamentals first: Is the product delivering on its promises? Are customers satisfied? Are we paying attention to their needs?

By honing in on the core issues, common-sense leaders can often solve problems faster and more effectively than those who chase sophisticated but unnecessary strategies. This ability to distill problems down to their simplest forms allows businesses to act quickly, minimize costs, and achieve results without overcomplicated approaches.

Practical example: A retail company noticing subpar in-store customer experience should initially focus on optimizing factors like store layout, staff training, and customer service, rather than hastily investing in expensive technological solutions to automate processes. Practical, cost-effective improvements, such as enhanced employee engagement and better product positioning, could yield immediate sales gains—showcasing the power of straightforward, logical solutions.

Experience-Based Judgment

Practical experience is the foundation of sound judgment, not just simplicity. Seasoned business leaders who have accumulated years of hands-on expertise cultivate a refined decision-making ability, allowing them to make well-informed choices without over-emphasizing data or theoretical frameworks. This experience-based judgment enables leaders to draw upon practical lessons learned from past victories and setbacks, rather than constantly starting from scratch.

This experience helps leaders:

- **Recognize patterns**: Experienced leaders who have navigated through various market conditions and competitive environments can often identify emerging trends that may escape the notice of less seasoned leaders. This ability enables them to anticipate potential problems or opportunities and take proactive measures before any issues escalate.
- **Learn from mistakes**: Leaders who have faced challenging choices comprehend what approaches were unsuccessful and the underlying reasons, enabling them to sidestep comparable pitfalls down the line. These perspectives, acquired through real-world experience, are priceless in grounding decision-making in practical realities, not just abstract concepts.

- **Remain adaptable**: Practical wisdom also encompasses the ability to adapt to evolving situations. Leaders with robust common sense recognize that just because a particular approach was successful previously, it may not necessarily be effective in the future. They are receptive to new insights and open to revising their perspectives as needed.

A leader's intuition, which is forged through experience, is frequently more valuable than a strict adherence to process or data. Experience enables leaders to look beyond the immediate issue, assess it from various perspectives, and recognize its long-term ramifications.

Practical example: An experienced CEO who has navigated through multiple economic recessions is able to handle a sudden decline in sales without panicking. Unlike younger leaders who may react hastily, this seasoned executive knows how to weather the storm. They focus on managing cash flow, making strategic cuts, and retaining their customer base. Their experience tells them that this temporary setback can be overcome if they approach it with a steady, level-headed approach, avoiding rash decisions that could potentially exacerbate the situation.

Balancing Data with Intuition

In today's business world, data-driven decision-making has become the standard. While data is undoubtedly valuable, it's important to recognize that not every decision can or should be based solely on data. There are times when the data is unclear, contradictory, or overwhelming, and leaders must rely on their intuition to fill in the gaps.

Common sense helps leaders know when to trust their instincts. This doesn't mean ignoring data; rather, it's about using data as one tool among many. Successful leaders understand that data provides insight, but intuition – built on years of experience – often identifies risks or opportunities that the numbers alone cannot reveal. Sometimes, gut feelings can detect emerging trends, recognize when something feels off, or predict customer responses in ways that quantitative models cannot.

Furthermore, data can often be manipulated or misinterpreted, leading to false conclusions. Leaders with common sense know how to discern when data should be trusted and when it might be skewing their judgment. They also understand that over-reliance on data can lead to "analysis paralysis," where too much time is spent reviewing numbers instead of taking action. Common sense allows leaders to strike a balance between informed decision-making and timely action.

Practical example: Envision a product manager assessing a novel marketing strategy. Although the statistics demonstrate that customer segments are positively engaging with the existing messaging, the manager's intuitive understanding - cultivated through extensive customer interactions over the years - indicates the need for a minor adjustment in tone or content. Their intuitive judgment proves accurate, and the revised campaign connects more effectively with a wider audience.

Simplicity in Communication and Strategy

Effective communication is the essence of common sense in business. Leaders should avoid using overly complicated jargon or convoluted explanations that make strategies difficult for people to comprehend and implement.

Business leaders who apply common sense recognize that if people don't understand the message, they cannot take meaningful action. Communication should be straightforward, concise, and focused on the essential points.

In strategy meetings, leaders who cut through unnecessary complexity are far more successful in rallying their teams around a common goal. When strategies are communicated simply, teams are more likely to be aligned, understand the key objectives, and execute efficiently. On the other hand, language heavy in jargon tends to create confusion and can alienate employees who are unfamiliar with certain terminologies.

Simplicity does not mean oversimplifying; it means getting to the core of what truly matters and ensuring that everyone, from entry-level employees to top executives, can follow the vision and contribute. By using plain language and focusing on actionable goals, leaders foster buy-in and build greater cohesion across their teams.

Practical example: A business implementing a new sales approach should use plain language instead of vague jargon like "synergy," "leveraging verticals," or "cross-functional alignments." Instead, they could state something direct, such as: "Our aim is to increase sales by 10% this quarter by contacting existing customers and broadening our product range." Straightforward, uncomplicated communication prompts action.

A Focus on People

At the core of any business are the people involved - the employees, customers, and stakeholders. It's simply common sense that treating these people fairly, building meaningful relationships with them, and focusing on solutions that cater to their needs are fundamental to a company's long-term success.

While data, processes, and technology are certainly important business elements, common sense reminds us that no amount of technological advancement or data analysis can replace the value of human intuition, motivation, and interpersonal skills. People are the most valuable asset in any business, and common sense dictates that fostering strong relationships and ensuring everyone feels valued and respected is crucial.

Leaders with common sense recognize the vital role of empathy, trust, and understanding in building strong, productive teams. They understand that employees who feel heard and appreciated are more likely to be loyal, innovative contributors. They also recognize that customers are more than just data points - they are people with real needs, and addressing those needs in a human-centered way is key to sustained business growth.

Practical example: A manager who makes the effort to hear their team out, comprehend their difficulties, and provide assistance is much more likely to cultivate a robust, unified group than one who concentrates solely on data and performance evaluations. By applying practical wisdom, they acknowledge that content, involved employees are the cornerstone of lasting achievement.

Case Example:

The story of Southwest Airlines showcases how common sense can drive success. Herb Kelleher, the company's founder, applied straightforward business strategies: prioritizing customer service, treating employees well, and streamlining operations. A prime example is Southwest's decision to utilize only the Boeing 737 aircraft. This simplified training, maintenance, and scheduling, ultimately reducing costs and enhancing service delivery. In essence, Southwest's triumph was largely propelled by pragmatic thinking.

Historical Examples of Common Sense in Business Success

To gain a deeper appreciation for the strength of practical wisdom, we can examine historical cases of business leaders and organizations that succeeded by employing straightforward, no-frills tactics. These examples demonstrate how uncomplicated, logical approaches have frequently proven more effective than overly complex or fashionable methods.

1. **Henry Ford's Assembly Line Innovation**:

Ford's implementation of the assembly line is a quintessential example of applying practical reasoning to business practices. Rather than making the manufacturing process more complex, Ford concentrated on streamlining it. He divided the car production process into straightforward, repetitive steps, enabling quicker output and reduced costs. The outcome was the Model T, a vehicle that was accessible to the typical American, as well as a breakthrough in industrial production. Ford's triumph was not fueled by intricate tactics but by a pragmatic approach to enhancing efficiency.

2. **Walmart's Focus on Low Prices and Efficiency**:

Sam Walton grew Walmart into the world's leading retailer by adhering to straightforward, practical principles:

offering low prices, investing in logistics to optimize efficiency, and concentrating on serving customers in rural markets that competitors had overlooked. Rather than complexifying operations with excessive product variety or high-end items, Walmart prioritized providing customers with what they truly desired—reasonably priced goods, readily available. Walton's pragmatic, no-nonsense approach built a retail powerhouse that continues to flourish today.

3. **IKEA's Flat-Pack Furniture**:

IKEA's choice to sell furniture in flat-packs is a clear instance of practical thinking leading to innovation. Instead of dedicating resources to complex shipping techniques, IKEA concentrated on lowering expenses by enabling customers to put together their own furniture. This strategy streamlined logistics, reduced prices, and became one of the defining features of IKEA's business approach. It's a straightforward concept that tackled genuine issues and has resulted in worldwide success.

These examples illustrate that common sense is not about being risk-averse or maintaining the status quo; instead, it involves making choices grounded in practicality, simplicity, and a clear grasp of human requirements.

Common Sense vs. Corporate Terminology

One of the reasons practical thinking has diminished in many business environments is the growing reliance on specialized jargon and overly technical language. As companies expand and industries become more specialized, the language used in corporate settings has become more complex. Business jargon can create an illusion of expertise or innovation, but it often obscures the simple truths and practical solutions that common sense would reveal.

Consider terms like "synergize," "low-hanging fruit," or "strategic alignment." While these phrases may sound impressive, they often obscure the real issues. Common sense dictates that clear communication is vital, especially in decision-making and strategy implementation. If teams don't understand what's being asked of them, confusion reigns, and execution falters.

Business jargon can also lead to overly complicated solutions. Leaders may feel pressure to introduce complex strategies because they sound more sophisticated. But in reality, the simplest solutions are often the most effective. For example, instead of discussing "leveraging core competencies to maximize stakeholder engagement," a common-sense approach might say: "Let's focus on what we're good at and listen to what our customers want."

The danger of jargon in decision-making is that it clouds understanding, encourages complexity, and distances leadership from the day-to-day realities of the business. Employees feel disconnected from high-level decisions if they don't understand them, and this erodes trust and engagement. Common sense, on the other hand, values transparency, simplicity, and straightforward communication.

Case Example:

A tech startup aiming to expand might get caught up in a cycle of using trendy industry terms like "disruptive innovation" and "pivoting" without addressing the fundamental issues of customer satisfaction or product quality. A leader who applies practical thinking would focus on ensuring that the product solves genuine problems for customers, the team is driven, and operations are functioning efficiently, steering clear of the trap of strategy sessions filled with jargon that don't lead to tangible results.

The Value of Common Sense Today

In today's rapidly evolving business environment, practical wisdom has become more valuable than ever. The relentless pace of technological change, global competition, and the overwhelming availability of data has created a world where complexity can easily obscure effective decision-making. Businesses are often tempted to chase the latest innovations, adapt to new tools, or gather endless data, mistakenly believing that more complexity leads to better outcomes. However, this pursuit of complexity can easily lead businesses astray, wasting precious time, money, and human resources on efforts that are not aligned with practical, sustainable growth.

Instead, businesses that embrace simplicity, focus on people, and trust practical judgment are better equipped to thrive in the long term. Practical wisdom helps leaders cut through the noise, filter out distractions, and keep their organizations focused on what truly matters. By making decisions that are rooted in experience and guided by a practical understanding of human nature, businesses can avoid the pitfalls of overcomplication and position themselves for ongoing success.

Let's further explore the critical insights for businesses aiming to reintegrate practical wisdom into their organizational culture and operations.

1. Keep It Simple: Focus on Clear, Actionable Strategies

In a business landscape filled with intricate models, multi-layered strategies, and complex technological solutions, it's easy for organizations to lose sight of their fundamental objectives. However, simplicity offers clarity and focus. Common sense champions simplicity by encouraging leaders to prioritize strategies that are straightforward and actionable.

For instance, instead of launching an extensive, multi-faceted growth strategy with numerous contingencies, a common-sense approach would concentrate on more immediate, manageable goals—objectives that can be measured and adjusted over time based on real-world feedback. These strategies do not rely on excessive analysis or complex systems; they are direct and actionable.

Keeping things simple does not mean avoiding ambition or innovation. It means breaking down large, complex goals into smaller, more digestible pieces, focusing on actionable steps that can be achieved with the available resources. It also means maintaining a laser focus on what truly matters to the business: delivering value to customers, improving processes, and empowering employees.

A common-sense strategy could involve rethinking priorities: Instead of adopting every new technology that promises disruption, leaders can ask, "Does this tool solve a real problem for us? Is this innovation aligned with our core mission?" This approach avoids the shiny-object syndrome, where companies chase the latest trends without a clear understanding of how they fit into their overall business goals.

Case Example:

Trader Joe's, a thriving grocery chain, has achieved success by maintaining a remarkably straightforward business approach. Instead of attempting to match the vast product selection of larger supermarkets, Trader Joe's concentrates on offering a carefully curated assortment of high-quality goods, many of which are their own private-label brands. This simplicity enables the company to lower costs, cultivate a unique customer experience, and sidestep the operational challenges of managing an expansive inventory of thousands of items.

2. Communicate Effectively: Avoid Jargon and Prioritize Transparency

In today's corporate environment, communication has often become overly complicated, filled with specialized terms, buzzwords, and corporate language that obscures meaning rather than clarifying it. Common sense emphasizes the need for clear, direct communication - both internally with teams and externally with customers, partners, and stakeholders.

Communication, especially at the leadership level, should prioritize clarity and transparency. Leaders who communicate in simple, understandable terms build trust and foster an environment where teams feel aligned with the company's mission and goals. In contrast, businesses that rely on complex, jargon-heavy language risk alienating their employees and creating a disconnect between leadership and the workforce.

Avoiding jargon isn't just about simplifying speech - it's about cultivating an open, honest culture where everyone, from entry-level employees to senior executives, understands the company's direction. Transparency in communication ensures that employees can align their actions with organizational goals, know what's expected of them, and feel empowered to contribute meaningfully.

Effective communication also extends to how businesses interact with customers and stakeholders. Customers value transparency, and businesses that communicate openly about their practices, pricing, and products often enjoy higher levels of trust and loyalty. In a competitive business landscape, clear and honest communication is a powerful differentiator.

Case Example:

Southwest Airlines is a prime example of a company that has made effective, straightforward communication a fundamental part of its values. Internally, they prioritize simplicity and clear messaging, steering clear of complex corporate language and ensuring that every employee, from pilots to customer service representatives, comprehends the company's mission and objectives. Externally, Southwest communicates with its customers in a friendly, direct manner, which fosters rapport and loyalty.

3. Trust Experience: Leverage the Lessons Learned from Past Successes and Failures

Common sense is deeply rooted in decision-making based on prior experience. In the rush to embrace new technologies and strategies, businesses often overlook the value of institutional knowledge and past experiences. Leaders with common sense understand that history frequently holds valuable lessons, and learning from past successes and failures can prevent costly mistakes in the future.

The business world is filled with trends and fads that promise groundbreaking results. However, those who apply common sense recognize that the most sustainable growth often comes from building upon what already works, rather than abandoning proven methods in favor of untested innovations. This is not to suggest that businesses should avoid new ideas, but rather that they should approach them with a healthy degree of skepticism, understanding that not all change equates to progress.

By relying on experience, leaders can evaluate opportunities more effectively. They can look back on similar situations to understand what worked, what didn't, and why. Leaders who leverage their experience are more likely to recognize patterns, anticipate challenges, and make decisions that are grounded in reality, not just theory.

Case Example:

Apple's decision to concentrate on a select range of premium products rather than competing in every market segment reflects their experience-based judgment. Apple's leadership, especially Steve Jobs, recognized early on that by focusing on a few core products—such as the iPhone, iPad, and Mac—they could dedicate more resources to refining their design, functionality, and customer experience. This focused approach, rooted in their past achievements, has contributed to Apple becoming one of the most valuable companies globally.

4. Empower People: Encourage Employees to Use Their Judgment and Solve Problems Practically

One of the most powerful aspects of common sense in business is its emphasis on enabling employees to think independently and address issues pragmatically. In many organizations, excessively rigid structures and micromanagement can stifle creativity and slow down decision-making. Common sense advocates for delegating authority and trusting employees to make decisions based on their experience and understanding of the situation.

By empowering people, businesses can tap into a wealth of practical wisdom and foster a culture of ownership. Employees who feel trusted to make decisions are more engaged, more innovative, and more likely to go the extra mile for the company. They become problem-solvers rather than simply following orders, which not only boosts productivity but also enhances job satisfaction ad retention.

Empowering employees also helps businesses remain agile. In fast-changing environments, waiting for decisions to move up and down the organizational hierarchy can lead to missed opportunities or slow responses to market changes. Common sense encourages businesses to flatten hierarchies where appropriate, granting employees the autonomy to act quickly and decisively when it matters most.

Case Example:

The renowned Ritz-Carlton hotel brand is renowned for its approach of empowering employees to provide exceptional customer service. Regardless of their role, each employee is entrusted with a discretionary budget to resolve customer issues immediately, whether that involves offering a complimentary night's lodging or arranging special accommodations. This trust placed in employees not only delights customers but also fosters a culture where staff feel empowered to make decisions that uphold the company's core values.

Chapter 2: The Erosion of Common Sense

As the business environment has undergone changes, a straightforward, practical approach to decision-making has gradually diminished. This decline can be attributed to several intricate factors, such as the emergence of a data-driven culture, heightened specialization, the advent of technology, and a growing preoccupation with innovation. While these elements have their merits, they have led many organizations to forsake direct, experience-based decision-making in favor of overly complex solutions and theoretical frameworks.

Information Overload: The Curse of Big Data

One of the primary factors driving the decline of practical reasoning is the overwhelming abundance of information. In the past, business executives made choices based on a combination of personal experience, industry expertise, and intuition. Yet, the proliferation of big data has dramatically altered the decision-making process, compelling leaders to support every decision with a vast trove of statistics and analytics. Although data can be a valuable asset for business expansion, its excessive reliance can actually conceal the most straightforward and efficient solutions.

1. **The Shift from Experience to Data Dependence**:

Data-driven decision-making has become a central focus for many organizations, with leaders frequently favoring analytics over their own personal judgment. Although this approach can provide valuable insights, an excessive dependence on data often results in "analysis paralysis"—a situation where the sheer volume of information prevents leaders from making decisions. Instead of relying on their intuition or expertise, leaders become preoccupied with the notion that every decision must be supported by intricate metrics.

2. **Data vs. Practicality**:

This heavy emphasis on data often comes at the expense of practical reasoning. In many situations, the most straightforward solution is the right one, but leaders get weighed down by excessive analysis and numerical rationalizations. When time is of the essence, spending extended periods crunching numbers can result in missed chances and indecision. For instance, a retail company that spends months studying whether to open a new location might miss out on a prime real estate chance simply because they were waiting for the ideal data model to justify the decision.

3. **Misinterpretation of Data**:

Data, although beneficial, is only as useful as the interpretation that underlies it. In numerous instances, businesses misinterpret data, resulting in flawed decision-making. A practical approach would question whether the data accurately represents the on-the-ground reality. Are customers genuinely abandoning a product due to pricing, or is it because the product itself is not meeting their needs? Numerical data can provide insights, but it rarely conveys the complete narrative. Common sense enables leaders to look beyond the numbers and comprehend the human factors driving those figures.

Case Example:

Once a leading player in the smartphone market, BlackBerry's downfall can be attributed to their failure to adapt to the changing industry landscape. BlackBerry primarily catered to enterprise customers, overlooking the growing popularity of consumer-focused smartphones. Despite evidence that business users valued security and functionality, BlackBerry disregarded the clear market demand for intuitive, touchscreen interfaces. Their inability to act on this seemingly obvious trend ultimately contributed to their rapid downfall.

The Rise of Overcomplication: When Simple Solutions Are Ignored

As organizations have become more intricate, there has been a rising tendency to make processes and decisions overly complicated. Leaders frequently feel compelled to implement elaborate, multi-faceted strategies, believing that complexity equates to sophistication or success. However, these convoluted solutions can obscure the straightforward, practical answers that intuition would otherwise bring to light.

1. **Complicated Strategies Over Straightforward Ones**:

Many organizations now prefer complex business models filled with technical terminology and intricate methods. These approaches may appear impressive, but they frequently fall short when it comes to implementation. Common sense suggests that the most effective strategy is often the simplest one—focus on what works, prioritize customer needs, and ensure that employees are empowered to take action.

For instance, instead of implementing a burdensome, multi-step process for handling customer feedback, a common-sense approach might emphasize direct communication with customers, empowering frontline employees to address issues immediately. This not only enhances customer satisfaction but also reduces the inefficiencies associated with complex hierarchies and approval procedures.

2. **The Illusion of Control through Complexity**:

Many leaders associate complexity with control, believing that more detailed plans and intricate strategies will lead to better results. However, in reality, complex decision-making processes frequently creates bottlenecks, suppresses innovation, and frustrates employees who must navigate through excessive bureaucracy. This false sense of control is harmful because it separates leadership from the actual issues, resulting in a disconnect between strategy and implementation.

3. **Simplicity as a Competitive Advantage**:

Simplicity is a defining characteristic of practical wisdom and can be a formidable competitive edge. In an environment where companies are frequently weighed down by excessively intricate systems and procedures, those that optimize their operations and concentrate on fundamental business tenets are better equipped to thrive. Enterprises that streamline their products and services, eliminate superfluous management levels, and prioritize efficient problem-solving frequently outshine their more convoluted counterparts.

Case Example:

Toyota's manufacturing approach showcases the power of practical, straightforward principles. Their Kaizen philosophy, which emphasizes gradual, ongoing enhancements, is founded on simple, incremental adjustments that drive productivity and quality. Instead of deploying overly intricate systems, Toyota empowers its workforce to identify inefficiencies and implement improvements in real-time. This mindset has enabled Toyota to become one of the most efficient and dependable automotive producers globally.

The Disconnect Between Academia and Real-World Business

Another factor that contributes to the decline of practical reasoning in business is the disconnect between academic concepts and real-world implementation. Business programs frequently teach intricate models, frameworks, and theories, many of which are based on idealized situations rather than the complex realities of managing an organization. Consequently, business executives who have been educated in these academic settings may find it challenging to apply practical, common-sense approaches in their day-to-day activities.

1. **Theoretical Models vs. Practical Solutions**:

Many business concepts can be beneficial in controlled settings, but they don't always transfer seamlessly to practical, real-world applications. For instance, SWOT analysis may help structure strategic thought processes, seasoned leaders recognize that the ability to adapt and respond to evolving circumstances is often more crucial than strictly adhering to rigid frameworks. Theoretical models can serve as useful guidelines, but practical wisdom ensures that leaders remain flexible and firmly rooted in the present context.

2. **Business Terminology and Complexity from Academic Contexts:**

Academic teachings frequently highlight intricate terminology and abstract ideas that, while mentally engaging, don't always connect with employees working on the ground. When leaders use these specialized terms, they risk distancing their teams, who may not fully grasp the high-level jargon. Practical wisdom prioritizes clarity in communication, ensuring that everyone in the organization, from senior executives to frontline staff, can comprehend and implement strategic choices.

3. **Lack of Focus on Human Factors**:

Academic models frequently concentrate on statistics, frameworks, and systems, but they overlook the human dimension of business—the feelings, motivations, and connections that propel employee productivity and customer devotion. Intuition acknowledges that people, not systems, are the foundation of every thriving enterprise. Leaders who use intuition prioritize cultivating robust relationships, empowering teams, and comprehending the needs and aspirations of their clientele.

Case Example:

Consider the case of Blockbuster, which failed to adapt to the rise of streaming services like Netflix. From an academic standpoint, Blockbuster's executives could rationalize their resistance to digital transformation through various business strategies and financial forecasts. However, a common-sense approach would have highlighted the clear trend: consumers favored the convenience of streaming over physical video rentals. Blockbuster's focus on preserving its existing business model, while disregarding evolving customer preferences, ultimately led to its downfall.

Innovation at the Expense of Practicality

While innovation is crucial for business expansion, the fixation on continuous disruption and originality has, in numerous instances, led organizations to forsake fundamental principles in pursuit of the newest fads. Practical wisdom does not dismiss innovation—it embraces it, but solely when it corresponds with the company's long-term objectives and practical requirements.

1. **Chasing Trends without Purpose**:

In the current business landscape, there is significant pressure to be at the forefront, to embrace the newest technologies, or to follow emerging patterns. Yet, organizations frequently jump on these trends without considering whether these innovations genuinely address any real issues. Prudence advises leaders to scrutinize new ideas carefully, posing questions such as: "Does this trend genuinely benefit our customers or employees? Is it aligned with our fundamental principles?"

2. **Disruption for Disruption's Sake**:

The emergence of the "disruptor" mentality has caused many organizations to prioritize change for its own sake, without thoroughly examining the potential consequences. While a certain degree of disruption is essential for development, blindly pursuing disruption can result in pandemonium and lack of clarity. Conversely, practicality encourages stability, recognizing that disruption must be counterbalanced with continuity and dependability. Not all sectors require a complete overhaul, and not every innovative concept merit implementation.

3. **Forgetting the Fundamentals**:

In the pursuit of innovation, numerous companies overlook the essential principles that underpin success—providing value to customers, caring for employees, and operating in a streamlined manner. Even the most groundbreaking businesses must remember these fundamental tenets. No level of technology or disruption can substitute the significance of cultivating trust with customers and fostering a positive work environment.

Case Example:

WeWork, once the golden child of the startup ecosystem, aggressively pursued rapid growth and innovation, seeking to transform the office space industry. However, the company failed to prioritize basic business principles: developing sustainable financial strategies, optimizing operations, and maintaining transparent communication with its stakeholders. WeWork's breakneck expansion and overvalued public perception ultimately resulted in the company teetering on the brink of collapse, serving as a cautionary tale about the perils of prioritizing innovation over practical business fundamentals.

Why Overcomplication Is Hurting Business Success

The erosion of practical reasoning in the business world has led to an environment where overcomplicated processes, excessive analysis, and heavy reliance on data have become the norm. While these tools and strategies have their place, they should not replace sound judgment. In fact, the most successful businesses are often the ones that prioritize simplicity, rely on practical experience, and maintain a clear connection to their core principles.

This chapter has highlighted how the decline of common sense—driven by information overload, the rise of complexity, academic theory, and innovation at the expense of practicality—has created significant challenges for modern organizations. To reclaim their agility and focus, businesses must reintroduce practical reasoning into their decision-making processes. By keeping things simple, focusing on people, and trusting practical judgment, companies can overcome the complexity that too often obscures their path to success.

Chapter 3: The Cost of Ignoring Common Sense

The diminishing role of common sense in the business world is not merely an academic or conceptual matter - it has tangible repercussions that can significantly impact an organization's operations, financial well-being, and overall culture. When common sense is disregarded in favor of complexity, excessive analysis, or following trends, businesses face a multitude of challenges. In this chapter, we will explore the real-world costs associated with sidelining common sense, from its effects on leadership effectiveness and employee productivity to its financial and operational ramifications. Through case studies and practical examples, this chapter aims to demonstrate why reintegrating common sense into the decision-making process is crucial for an organization's long-term success.

The Human Factor: How the Lack of Common Sense Impacts Employees

In any organization, employees are the driving force behind its success. When their needs and perspectives are overlooked, it directly impacts their productivity, engagement, and overall morale. A business culture that prioritizes complexity, rigid structures, and excessive analysis often leads to confusion, frustration, and a lack of motivation among the workforces. Common sense suggests that employees should be empowered to use their own judgment and experience to make decisions and solve problems. Yet, in many organizations, this fundamental principle is often disregarded.

1. **Overcomplicated Processes and Bureaucracy**:

One of the most evident ways that a lack of practical reasoning is exhibited in the workplace is through excessively complex processes. Employees are frequently compelled to navigate through endless bureaucratic layers and approval channels just to accomplish even basic tasks. Rather than being able to act swiftly and decisively, they are weighed down by a system that prioritizes protocols over results.

Example: Visualize a scenario where an employee is attempting to address a customer's concern, but instead of being granted the authority to make an on-the-spot decision, they are obligated to escalate the issue through various levels of management for approval. This process delays the resolution and leaves both the employee and the customer feeling frustrated. Logically, it would make sense for frontline employees to be trusted to autonomously handle routine problems, which would enhance both productivity and customer satisfaction.

2. Employee Frustration and Low Morale:

When workers are exposed to unneeded intricacy and strict procedures, it fosters aggravation. They frequently feel constrained, unable to act based on their own judgment or address the genuine demands of their position. This lack of empowerment leads to low morale and detachment. Employees become less invested in their work because they feel their capacity to make a difference is restricted.

Example: In numerous large organizations, the ability to innovate is hindered because workers at junior levels are not granted the liberty to experiment with new concepts without navigating a labyrinth of approvals. A practical solution would foster a culture of exploration and confidence, enabling employees to present novel ideas without the concern of becoming entangled in bureaucratic obstacles.

3. The Erosion of Trust and Autonomy:

Trusted employees are essential for a thriving workplace. When managers fail to have confidence in their staff's decision-making abilities, it leads to a breakdown in trust between employees and leadership. This often results in excessive micromanagement, leaving the organization with a disengaged workforce that is reluctant to go the extra mile. Logic dictates that when given the freedom to exercise their judgment, employees will typically rise to the challenge and take pride in their work. However, in environments where power is highly centralized and organizational structures are inflexible, that critical element of trust tends to deteriorate.

Example: A company that introduces a new project management software to monitor every tiny aspect of an employee's work may believe it's enhancing productivity. Yet, logical reasoning would suggest that employees are likely to feel excessively controlled and under constant surveillance, diminishing their independence and hindering their creativity. Over the long run, this results in a lack of innovation and a drop in job fulfillment.

Financial Pitfalls: The High Cost of Overcomplication

Prioritizing complexity and excessive analysis over practical reasoning can negatively affect not only employee morale, but also have significant financial repercussions. Companies that favor theoretical approaches, excessive data scrutiny, or chasing the latest trends often end up squandering substantial financial resources on initiatives that fail to deliver tangible value. The price of disregarding common sense manifests in the form of wasted time, inefficient operations, and missed chances for growth.

1. **Wasted Resources on Unnecessary Complexity**:

Organizations that make their processes, systems, and decision-making overly complex often invest a disproportionate amount of money on consultants, tools, and technologies that may not be essential. Although these investments are frequently justified as necessary for innovation or optimization, the actual cost is that many of these systems and processes do not enhance the bottom line - they merely add layers of complexity.

Example: Many organizations implement enterprise resource planning (ERP) or customer relationship management (CRM) systems that are more advanced than their actual requirements. The implementation costs, along with the ongoing training and maintenance expenses, can add up to millions of dollars. A more practical approach would be to adopt simpler and more cost-effective systems that fulfill the organization's needs without introducing unnecessary complexity.

2. **Opportunity Costs of Analysis Paralysis**:

Excessive dependence on data and analysis frequently results in missed chances. In rapidly evolving markets, the capacity to act swiftly and decisively can be a crucial competitive edge. However, businesses that are perpetually waiting for the "ideal" data before making choices often fall behind more nimble competitors. The price of inaction, or being paralyzed by analysis, can be enormous, particularly in sectors where being the first mover is crucial.

Example: A retail company that spends an extensive amount of time scrutinizing customer data before deciding to enter a new market may miss the chance entirely, as competitors act more rapidly. Intuition suggests that businesses don't always necessitate 100% certainty before taking action—occasionally, a well-thought-out, timely decision based on 80% of the data is significantly more valuable than a flawless decision made too late.

3. **Innovation vs. Practicality: The Cost of Chasing Trends**:

Many organizations waste resources by pursuing the most recent industry fads or embracing disruptive technologies without fully comprehending their consequences. While innovation is crucial, prudence dictates that businesses should verify that any new technology or trend aligns with their practical needs and long-term objectives before investing significantly. Chasing innovation for its own sake can result in wasted financial resources and operational inefficiencies.

Example: General Electric (GE) serves as a prime example of a company that faced difficulties due to its pursuit of numerous innovations without grounding them in practical considerations. Under the leadership of former CEO Jeff Immelt, GE invested substantial resources into futuristic projects such as the "Industrial Internet of Things," without a clear path to profitability. These investments failed to yield the expected returns, leading GE to divest many of these initiatives at a loss. A more prudent approach would have been to carefully assess whether these technologies were realistically aligned with GE's core competencies and customer needs before committing significant resources to these endeavors.

Corporate Culture and Decision Paralysis: The Cost of Poor Leadership

The culture of an organization is often shaped by the behavior and decision-making patterns of its leaders. Leaders who make overly complicated choices, delay actions due to excessive analysis, or pursue impractical strategies can cultivate a culture of stagnation and inaction. This is one of the most significant hidden costs of disregarding practical wisdom: when leadership is bogged down in complexity, the entire organization bears the impact.

1. **Leaders Who Overanalyze and Overcomplicate**:

In organizations where leaders are reluctant to make decisions without having absolute certainty, the pace of progress becomes extremely slow. The persistent demand for additional data, more research, and further validation leads to a decision-making process that is sluggish and unwieldy. This not only affects the speed of business operations but also undermines the confidence of employees, who may perceive the leadership as lacking decisiveness.

Example: A CEO who demands extensive market research and comprehensive scenario planning before approving a new product rollout may cause the company to waste precious time. Meanwhile, more agile competitors have already introduced similar offerings and claimed a portion of the market. A pragmatic leader would strike a balance between the need for thorough investigation and the need for timely decision-making, acknowledging that no decision can ever be made with 100% certainty.

2. **The Domino Effect of Poor Leadership**:

Poor leadership choices don't just impact the upper levels of an organization—their effects ripple down through the entire company, affecting all operational levels. When leaders implement intricate, impractical strategies, it sows confusion among managers and employees, who then have to adhere to convoluted procedures that may not even support the company's objectives. This cascading impact leads to inefficiency, disarray, and ultimately, a lack of cohesion across the organization.

3. **Decision Paralysis and Missed Opportunities**:

Indecisiveness is one of the most detrimental consequences of ineffective leadership. When leaders fail to make prompt, practical choices, valuable opportunities are lost, and competitors are swift to capitalize on them. Furthermore, this fosters an environment where employees are reluctant to take risks or make decisions autonomously, fearing repercussions for acting without extensive research or authorization. Rational thinking dictates that businesses must strike a balance between strategic planning and action, and leaders should foster a culture that promotes proactive decision-making.

Example: A major company that fails to evolve with the digital transformation movement due to its leadership being mired in endless discussions about whether it's the appropriate course of action may discover itself playing catch-up with more agile competitors. By the time the decision is made, the market landscape may have already shifted, leaving the organization fighting an uphill battle to remain competitive.

Long-Term Organizational Risks: Eroding Resilience and Agility

The long-term well-being of an organization can be severely impacted by disregarding practical wisdom. Businesses that favor intricacy over simplicity, excessive analysis over prompt decision-making, and fads over core principles, jeopardize their ability to withstand challenges and adapt quickly—which are two crucial qualities for enduring success in today's unpredictable and competitive business landscape.

1. **Loss of Organizational Agility**:

Organizations that are bogged down in complexity and excessive analysis lose their agility to respond swiftly to shifting market conditions. On the other hand, common sense promotes adaptability and prompt decision-making. Businesses that embrace common-sense approaches are more flexible and better prepared to manage market disruptions, as they steer clear of the inaction resulting from overly convoluted procedures.

2. **Erosion of Customer Trust**:

When companies implement impractical and overly intricate solutions, it frequently results in inconsistent experiences for their customers. Customers appreciate simplicity - whether in the products and services offered, the customer support provided, or the communication channels used. If organizations make their internal operations unnecessarily complex, customers are left feeling frustrated and may start to doubt the reliability of the brand. It is simply logical that businesses should always focus on facilitating clear, straightforward, and efficient interactions with their customers in order to cultivate long-lasting loyalty.

Why Businesses Must Reintroduce Common Sense

Disregarding practical wisdom in business can have profound implications. From undermining employee morale and productivity to squandering financial resources and missing crucial opportunities, the repercussions are far-reaching. Leaders who prioritize complexity and excessive analysis over practicality risk cultivating a culture of confusion, stagnation, and unrealized potential.

By reintroducing common sense into their leadership and operations, businesses can enhance their agility, boost employee engagement, reduce operational inefficiencies, and bolster customer trust. Ultimately, common sense is not merely a useful tool, but a necessity for survival and long-term success in today's fast-paced business landscape.

Chapter 4: Rediscovering Common Sense

After examining the consequences of disregarding practical wisdom, it's crucial for businesses to rediscover and reintegrate it into their operations and decision-making processes. This chapter will provide practical strategies to simplify decision-making, balance data with intuition, and trust experience over complex, theoretical approaches. Businesses that commit to rediscovering practical wisdom can cut through the clutter of modern corporate culture, improve efficiency, empower their employees, and ultimately achieve sustainable success. The core message here is that practical wisdom is not something to be abandoned in the face of data, innovation, or complexity—it is a tool that should be embraced to ground decisions in practicality, experience, and human insight.

Embracing Simplicity in Decision-Making

One of the most efficient methods to regain practical wisdom in business is to adopt simplicity—particularly in the decision-making process. Business executives frequently believe that intricate issues necessitate intricate solutions, but this isn't always accurate. Over-complicating decisions can result in analysis paralysis, perplexity, and ineffectiveness.

1. **Streamlining Decision Processes**:

Simple, straightforward processes typically result in faster, more effective decision-making. To cultivate simplicity, organizations should minimize redundant approval steps and give decision-making authority to employees at all levels. When leaders trust their teams to act based on clear, uncomplicated guidelines, they enable a more responsive and nimble organization.

Example: Rather than mandating that every decision pass through numerous committees or senior leadership groups, organizations should grant middle managers the authority to make choices on behalf of their respective departments. For instance, at Zappos (an American shoe & clothing retailer), the customer service team is empowered to resolve customer problems immediately without the need to escalate to management. This straightforward, logical approach leads to more satisfied customers and more engaged employees.

2. **The Power of Delegation**:

One of the defining characteristics of practical and sensible leadership is the ability to effectively delegate tasks and responsibilities. Leaders who insist on personally overseeing every decision made within the organization end up slowing down the entire operation and suppressing the empowerment of their employees. A practical and reasonable approach to leadership promotes delegation, enabling leaders to concentrate on the most crucial matters while having confidence in their teams to manage routine, day-to-day decisions.

Example: Netflix has constructed its organizational culture on a basis of trust and autonomy. Employees are granted the freedom to make substantial decisions within their respective domains without the need for excessive oversight. By delegating decision-making power, Netflix has cultivated a highly adaptable and creative workforce.

3. **Simplifying Strategy**:

Strategies that are straightforward and concentrated tend to be more effective than those weighed down by an excess of objectives, metrics, and initiatives. Sound judgment suggests that companies should prioritize core aims and develop strategies that are clear and easy to execute. A sensible strategy also allows for adaptability—the ability to respond to market shifts without overly complicating the decision-making process.

Example: Southwest Airlines achieved success by embracing a simple business approach. The decision to utilize a single aircraft type, the Boeing 737, enabled the airline to streamline its maintenance, training, and operational processes. This straightforward strategy resulted in cost savings, enhanced efficiency, and greater customer satisfaction.

Balancing Data with Intuition

Although data is an invaluable resource in the contemporary business landscape, common sense dictates that not every decision should rely solely on data-driven analysis. There are instances where data alone may prove inadequate, ambiguous, or even potentially misleading. The most accomplished leaders understand when to strike a balance between data-driven insights and their own intuition and expertise.

1. **Data as a Tool, Not a Crutch**:

In our current data-centric society, it can be tempting to solely depend on numerical information when making choices. Yet, logic dictates that data is merely one component of the bigger picture. Skilled decision-makers leverage data as a resource to guide their judgment, but do not allow it to completely determine their actions. At times, leaders must make choices based on partial or unclear data, drawing upon their instincts to supplement the missing information.

Example: Steve Jobs was renowned for relying on his intuition when creating Apple products such as the iPhone. Although market analysis indicated that consumers favored physical keyboards, Jobs intuitively believed that a touchscreen interface would be more groundbreaking. His decision to trust his instincts rather than the data resulted in one of the most iconic and successful products ever made.

2. **Avoiding Data Overload**:

With access to more data than ever before, many businesses face data overload, which can lead to paralysis or confusion. We can deduce from common sense that not all data is relevant, and trying to examine every bit of information frequently results in overcomplication. Rather, companies ought to focus on the most relevant data that supports their objectives, leaving space for experience and gut feeling to influence choices.

Example: Despite Amazon is well known for its significant use of data, intuition is also highly valued by the corporation. For instance, there wasn't much data available when Amazon decided to establish its Prime membership service. Even if early data didn't show a sure return on investment, Jeff Bezos trusted his instincts that customers would value speedier shipping and additional benefits. At present, one of the most frequently used offerings offered by the company is Amazon Prime.

3. **When to Trust Your Gut**:

Common-sense leaders understand that information may not be accurate or thorough, and that when that happens, it's usually preferable to follow your instincts. It is important to understand when experience-honed instincts are more trustworthy than data points rather than disregarding data.

Example: Elon Musk frequently follows his instincts when making choices, particularly in the beginning when launching new businesses like SpaceX and Tesla. After several unsuccessful rocket launches, evidence indicated that SpaceX could need to shut down. Nonetheless, Musk kept the business going forward, which ultimately led to success, thanks to his common sense assessment of the possibility for future success and his instinct about the importance of persistence.

Trusting Experience: The Importance of Learning from the Past

Making decisions based on experience is the foundation of common sense. Leaders with a multitude of experience who have witnessed several market cycles, faced obstacles, and guided teams through achievements and setbacks are a great resource. Making decisions based on this experience rather than just theoretical models or outside advisors is generally more effective.

1. **Leveraging Past Experiences**:

Experience teaches us lessons that data alone cannot provide. Leaders who have faith in their experience are able to see patterns, foresee possible issues, and make well-founded decisions. Projections and data are useful, but nothing compares to the understanding that comes from actual experiences.

Example: The former CEO of Starbucks, Howard Schultz, knew when the company had overexpanded because of his experience building the company. In the end, Schultz's decision to slow down growth and focused on the customer experience helped the business return to profitability because he trusted his judgment and experience.

2. **Learning from Failure**:

Failure serves as a valuable instructor in the realm of business, and wise leaders acknowledge and learn from their errors. Rather than avoiding conversations about past failures, they assess them to enhance their future decision-making. Through experience, leaders can identify effective strategies from ineffective ones, and utilize these insights when faced with new challenges.

Example: Before creating the globally renowned Disney brand we know today, Walt Disney faced several business setbacks. Through endeavors such as Laugh-O-Gram Studios, he gained crucial insights into financial management, creativity, and tenacity, which he later applied to establish one of the most prosperous entertainment companies in the world.

3. **Building on What Works**:

Practical leaders do not start from scratch every time they face a challenge. Instead, they enhance established approaches and concentrate on making gradual improvements. This does not imply disregarding innovation, but it does involve acknowledging when current methods are effective and deciding to modify them only when essential.

Example: The Toyota production system exemplifies this concept well. Instead of implementing completely new systems for each innovation, Toyota enhances its lean manufacturing principles, consistently enhancing and perfecting them over time. By prioritizing gradual improvement through experience, the company has established itself as a frontrunner in efficiency and quality.

Empowering Employees with Common Sense Decision-Making

Empowering employees to make decisions based on their judgment and experience is a powerful method to rediscover common sense within an organization. An approach based on common sense entails granting employees the freedom to act within set guidelines, rather than micromanaging every aspect of their work with strict rules and processes.

1. **Decentralizing Decision-Making**:

Decentralization is encouraged by common sense, which permits decisions to be made at the level nearest to the issue. As a result, workers are empowered to take responsibility for their job and handle problems faster rather than waiting for higher-ups' approval. Workers that have a sense of empowerment are more enthusiastic, creative, and productive.

Example: Employees at Ritz-Carlton are granted a discretionary budget to address client issues immediately. Employees are empowered to handle guest complaints on their own, without needing to escalate them to management. This includes offering additional amenities or compensating the guest with a complimentary night's stay. High levels of employee engagement and customer satisfaction result from this sensible strategy.

2. **Encouraging Practical Problem-Solving**:

The people closest to the day-to-day operations and client contacts are frequently the employees. They are therefore in a great position to recognize workable solutions to issues. Encouraging staff members to solve problems on their own initiative rather than waiting for orders can greatly increase productivity and creativity within the company.

Example: Google encourages its workers to dedicate 20% of their workdays to projects that pique their interest. Employee creativity and inventive problem-solving are fostered by this freedom, which frequently results in breakthroughs that would not have happened under a more strict framework.

3. **Fostering a Culture of Trust and Accountability**:

A culture of trust and accountability is fostered by leaders who possess common sense. Employees take greater responsibility for their job and are more likely to be proactive in problem-solving when they are trusted to make judgments based on their judgment. Common-sense leaders establish clear rules and allow their teams to behave within those parameters, trusting them to make the correct judgments.

Example: The video game firm Valve does not have any official hierarchies in place. Workers are trusted to choose what they want to work on, coordinate projects with others, and efficiently manage their time. This culture of trust and rational decision-making has produced ground-breaking, inventive products.

Rediscovering Common Sense for a More Effective Business

It's critical to concentrate on how companies may reclaim and incorporate common sense back into their operations and decision-making processes after examining the consequences of doing otherwise. This chapter will offer helpful techniques for streamlining decision-making, striking a balance between facts and intuition, and putting experience ahead of sophisticated, theoretical frameworks. Companies that make a commitment to regaining common sense will be able to succeed over the long term by empowering their staff, increasing productivity, and slicing through the complexity of contemporary corporate culture. The main takeaway from this is that common sense is a valuable tool that should be used to inform judgments based on experience, human understanding, and pragmatism rather than being dismissed in the face of data, innovation, or complexity.

Chapter 5: Leading with Common Sense

One of the most important areas where common sense can have a significant impact is in leadership. This chapter delves into the ways in which leaders can foster a pragmatic and analytical perspective, so enabling their staff, streamlining tactics, and encouraging openness. Instead of micromanaging or making decisions from the top down, common sense leadership focuses on fostering an atmosphere where simple, workable solutions flourish, and staff members are empowered to make their own decisions. Common sense leadership is a powerful tool for creating trust, encouraging creativity, and achieving long-term success.

Common Sense Leadership: Simplicity and Clarity at the Helm

Common sense-based leadership emphasizes realism, simplicity, and clarity. Instead of overcomplicating matters to appear more strategic, common-sense leaders strive to break down complex challenges into their most basic elements and concentrate on coming up with sensible, doable solutions. A leader with common sense promotes a culture of action and problem-solving, where choices are made based on reality rather than theory.

1. **Cutting Through the Noise**:

Common sense-embodied leaders can break through the clutter of excessive complexity, over-analysis, and corporate jargon. They realize that simplicity entails clarity of thought and an emphasis on what important, not a lack of depth. This enables leaders to make decisions more quickly, communicate more clearly, and develop strategies that are easy for their people to implement.

Example: During her tenure as CEO of PepsiCo, Indra Nooyi streamlined the company's approach by concentrating on three primary areas: healthier products, sustainability, and a supportive work environment. Rather than pursuing numerous objectives, Nooyi employed practicality to prioritize these three foundations, making it simpler for the company to coordinate its endeavors and concentrate on specific, significant goals.

2. **Practical Thinking Over Theoretical Approaches**:

Common-sense leaders don't rely just on elaborate theories or models from academia; instead, they concentrate on what actually works in the real world. Although these frameworks can be useful for comprehending business environments, sensible executives are aware that each company is different and that choices should be made based on firsthand knowledge and expertise.

Example: The CEO of Berkshire Hathaway, Warren Buffett, is renowned for taking a practical approach to investing. Buffett bases his investing decisions on simple principles: he looks for companies with solid fundamentals, uncomplicated business models, and capable management. Many investors use sophisticated financial models. His methodology prioritizes long-term, pragmatic decision-making over ephemeral, theory-driven tactics.

3. **Leading by Example**:

Being a wise leader also means setting a good example. Loyalty and trust are fostered in a team by leaders who model these qualities. They don't only preach about streamlining procedures and reaching choices with clarity; they live these ideas out in their own leadership approach. As a result, a culture of confidence in leadership is fostered among the staff, and they are more inclined to use common sense themselves.

Example: The previous CEO of Ford, Alan Mulally, is a shining example of sensible leadership. Mulally came over Ford at a time when the business was beset by an oversized bureaucracy and a lackluster strategy. Mulally focused on developing a clear plan that all staff members could comprehend and adhere to, setting an example for the rest of the organization by streamlining its procedures. His uncomplicated, sensible strategy assisted Ford in avoiding bankruptcy and turning a profit again.

The Art of Communication: Clarity and Transparency

One of the most important abilities of a common-sense leader is effective communication. Clear and open communicators encourage cooperation, alignment, and trust among their teams. On the other hand, executives who communicate using a lot of language or in complex ways can cause misunderstandings and misalignment. Communicating with common sense involves making sure that messages are understandable, succinct, and pertinent to the target audience.

1. **Simplicity in Messaging**:

Simplifying communication is a hallmark of common-sense leadership. Effective communicators make it easier for their teams to comprehend the objectives of the company and how each member of the team fits into the bigger picture. Employees may concentrate on their task without worrying about the organization's priorities when there is clear communication.

Example: Apple CEO Tim Cook is renowned for his straightforward and uncomplicated communication approach. This is reflected in Apple's messaging, both outwardly and internally. Apple's leadership makes sure that important messages are clear whether presenting financial data or product strategies. This builds trust with customers, employees, and shareholders.

2. **Transparency Builds Trust**:

Leaders with common sense know that fostering trust within their businesses requires transparency. Employee engagement and alignment with the company's objectives are higher when executives are transparent about the opportunities and difficulties facing the organization. Transparency fosters a culture where employees feel free to voice issues and exchange ideas without worrying about the consequences.

Example: Under the direction of its creator, Yvon Chouinard, Patagonia (an outdoor clothing company) has established a transparent culture that permeates every aspect of the business. The executives of Patagonia have made it apparent that the company is dedicated to environmental sustainability, and they have experienced both the joys and the difficulties associated with realizing this goal. Customers and staff alike have developed a strong sense of loyalty and trust as a result of this openness.

3. **Communicating with Empathy**:

Empathy is a component of common sense communication in addition to clarity and transparency. Communicating in a way that really resonates with their team requires leaders to take the time to understand their viewpoints and concerns. Stronger relationships between managers and staff are forged via empathic communication, which boosts morale and collaboration.

Example: Microsoft CEO Satya Nadella is renowned for his compassionate management approach. Nadella highlighted the value of empathy in communication and decision-making when he assumed leadership of Microsoft. His straightforward and straightforward communication style, along with his common sense approach to comprehending employee needs, contributed to the transformation of Microsoft's culture into one of creativity and teamwork.

Empowering Teams Through Common-Sense Leadership

Leaders with common sense understand that their success is dependent upon others around them. One of the main tenets of common-sense leadership is enabling teams to make independent decisions and apply sound judgment when solving issues. Leaders cultivate a culture of accountability, creativity, and involvement by granting their staff members the freedom to decide for themselves and act independently.

1. **Decentralizing Decision-Making**:

Decentralizing decision-making is one of the best strategies for empowering teams. Leaders with common sense understand that those closest to the task are frequently in the best position to make wise decisions. Leaders create an agile, responsive company and free up time to focus on strategic concerns by delegating decision-making authority to managers and front-line staff.

Example: Customer service at Nordstrom, which is powered by a decentralized decision-making framework, has long been renowned. Supervisor consent is not required for choices made by front-line staff to address consumer concerns on the spot. This confidence in staff members fosters a culture that is strongly customer-focused and increases responsiveness.

2. **Encouraging Problem-Solving**:

Leaders with common sense create an environment where staff members are rewarded for taking the initiative to solve issues. Instead, than waiting for orders or permissions from higher-ups, staff are given the freedom to address issues as they arise. This not only enhances productivity but also helps staff develop their own problem-solving abilities and confidence.

Example: Employees of Gore-Tex's parent business, W.L. Gore & Associates, work in a flat, dispersed structure called a "lattice organization." Workers are given the freedom to solve problems on their own, without waiting for orders from higher-ups. The result of this sensible approach to empowerment is a highly creative and motivated staff.

3. **Balancing Autonomy with Accountability**:

While empowering their teams, sensible leaders strike a balance between accountability and autonomy. Allowing employees to make decisions on their own while still holding them accountable for the results is what is meant by empowering them. In addition to giving direction and ensuring that staff members have the tools they need to succeed, leaders also need to set clear expectations.

Example: Under Jack Welch, workers at General Electric (GE) were encouraged to experiment and take chances, but they were also responsible for producing results. Welch promoted autonomy and teamwork in his "boundaryless" company, but his well-known "rank and yank" system made sure that underachievers were held responsible. This strategy attracted criticism, but it also fostered a high-performance culture that emphasized accountability and creativity.

Case Studies of Leaders Who Get It Right

There are innumerable instances of business executives who exhibit common sense in their leadership approaches. By adhering to pragmatic, experience-based decision-making and transparent communication, these leaders have been able to achieve long-term success, inspire their teams, and completely change their businesses. Let's examine a few of these instances in more detail:

1. **Herb Kelleher (Southwest Airlines)**:

Co-founder and former CEO of Southwest Airlines Herb Kelleher was a master of practical leadership. From the airline's business model (which uses a single model of aircraft) to its customer service (which provides basic, cheap flights), he founded Southwest on the idea of simplicity. Kelleher concentrated on giving workers autonomy, allowing them to make decisions on a daily basis, and maintaining a clear and targeted organization strategy. His sensible strategy enabled Southwest Airlines—which is renowned for its high personnel morale and devoted clientele—to develop into one in the most prosperous airlines globally.

2. **Mary Barra (General Motors)**:

General Motors CEO Mary Barra has received recognition for her common sense approach to leadership, which blends an emphasis on innovation with pragmatic, experience-based decision-making. GM was dealing with serious issues when Barra became CEO, including the aftermath of a large-scale safety recall. Barra handled the situation by acting quickly and decisively and by being open and honest with the people. She streamlined GM's processes by concentrating on its core offerings and getting rid of pointless red tape, all the while encouraging her teams to think creatively about how automotive technology would develop in the future, especially with regard to electric vehicles.

3. **Richard Branson (Virgin Group)**:

The Virgin Group's founder, Richard Branson, is a shining example of a common-sense leader who has developed a diversified and prosperous corporate empire by putting people first and making calculated decisions. Branson is renowned for encouraging an innovative culture, giving his staff members a lot of freedom, and communicating in an open and transparent manner. He exhorts executives in his company to follow their gut feelings, take measured chances, and concentrate on the demands of the client. Virgin's success in a variety of businesses can be attributed in large part to Branson's emphasis on sensible leadership.

Building a Leadership Culture Grounded in Common Sense

Leadership driven by common sense is a powerful approach that enhances decision-making, encourages employee involvement, and strengthens organizations by making them more adaptable. Common-sense leaders create an environment conducive to the growth of their teams and the flourishing of innovation by prioritizing simplicity, clarity, transparency, and empowerment.

In today's rapidly changing business landscape, common-sense leadership is more crucial than ever. Leaders who strike a balance between data and intuition, decentralize decision-making, and communicate clearly and transparently are better equipped to tackle challenges and capitalize on opportunities. The key to long-term success lies in reconnecting with the practical, experience-based wisdom that common sense provides and applying it in a way that is responsive to both the business and its people's needs.

Chapter 6: Instilling Common Sense in Corporate Culture

Even while sensible leadership is essential to a company's success, incorporating common sense into the corporate culture makes sure that it permeates all aspect of the business's operations. The decisions, interactions, and approaches to problems that employees take on are influenced by the culture of the organization. Thus, cultivating a common sense culture involves more than just what leaders do; it also entails establishing an atmosphere where empowerment, simplicity, and common sense reasoning are valued at all organizational levels.

This chapter will look at how companies can create a high-performing, flexible, and sustainable culture by rewarding employees who make wise decisions, training staff to use good judgment, and hiring for practicality.

Hiring for Practicality: Bringing in Common-Sense Thinkers

Making sure the correct individuals are brought on board is one of the first stages in creating a culture of common sense. It is essential to hire workers that exhibit sound judgment, practical thinking, and a simplicity-focused approach. Hiring for common sense is finding candidates who can apply workable answers to real-world situations rather than only depending on theory or intricate procedures, even though technical abilities and qualifications are still crucial.

1. **Prioritizing Problem-Solving Skills in Recruitment**:

When hiring, organizations should look beyond academic credentials or specialized technical abilities. They should emphasize individuals who have proven actual problem-solving talents in past roles. This entails focusing interview questions on the candidate's use of sound judgment in challenging circumstances. For example, finding out how they handled a client issue, streamlined a procedure, or effectively and pragmatically handled a project.

Example: One of the main employment requirements at Southwest Airlines is looking for candidates that can solve challenges practically and with rapid thinking. They put a lot of effort into selecting workers that possess great initiative, can clearly communicate with customers, and are technically proficient. This strategy makes sure that new workers can adapt to the fast-paced, customer-focused atmosphere of the airline.

2. **Hiring for Cultural Fit**:

In addition to skills, it's important for businesses to prioritize hiring individuals whose values are in line with the company's culture. If the company values common sense, simplicity, and practicality, these should be considered in the hiring process. Leaders should evaluate how closely a candidate's mindset matches the culture they want to cultivate, particularly in terms of decision-making and teamwork.

Example: As a corporation well-known for its environmental activism, Patagonia puts a lot of focus on employing individuals who share its ideals. During the recruitment process, they look for individuals who are not just talented but also committed to practical, meaningful work in keeping with their goal. This keeps the company culture strong by ensuring that new hires bring common sense and passion to their responsibilities.

3. **Assessing Emotional Intelligence and Adaptability**:

In the workplace, common sense is frequently associated with emotional intelligence (EQ), which involves the capacity to comprehend and handle emotions, both personal and those of others. Individuals with strong EQ are usually more adept at resolving conflicts, making pragmatic choices during challenging circumstances, and working effectively with others. They are also highly adaptable, which is crucial for excelling in a culture driven by common sense, where decisions often require swift action and are influenced by evolving circumstances.

Example: Testing candidates for cultural fit, emotional intelligence, and flexibility is a significant step in the hiring process at Zappos. In addition to their task-solving skills, candidates are evaluated on how well they manage real-world situations that call for sound judgment and consumer empathy. This supports the business in upholding a proactive problem-solving and customer satisfaction culture.

Training for Common Sense: Developing Practical Decision-Making

Ensuring you have the right team in place is only the starting point. In order to integrate practical thinking into the company culture, it is essential to provide training that encourages employees to think critically and apply common-sense principles in their day-to-day tasks. This requires going beyond strict training manuals and concentrating on cultivating judgment, critical thinking, and problem-solving abilities that are in line with the company's objectives.

1. **Encouraging Critical Thinking and Judgment**:

The goal of common sense training is to provide staff members the skills they need to quickly evaluate situations and decide wisely given the information at hand. Businesses should teach employees to think critically about the issues they encounter and to trust their gut feelings when a simple solution is apparent, instead of depending exclusively on standard operating procedures.

Example: Nordstrom provides its employees with the ability to make decisions that prioritize the customer without strict adherence to a set of rules. The company's employee handbook is well-known for being concise, emphasizing the importance of exercising good judgment in every scenario. This straightforward training method helps employees feel assured in their ability to make decisions aligned with the company's values and practical reasoning.

2. **Scenario-Based Training**:

Rather than concentrating on theoretical models or classroom-style instruction, businesses should use scenario-based training to promote common sense in their workforce. Employees undergoing this kind of training are placed in practical settings where they must use sound judgment to solve challenges. Role-playing scenarios including leadership conundrums, team obstacles, or customer service concerns can all promote prompt, efficient decision-making.

Example: Starbucks employs scenario-based training to assist baristas in managing various situations, such as addressing customer complaints and handling high-stress periods during busy hours. Through simulating these scenarios, Starbucks guarantees that employees are able to promptly evaluate and resolve issues using their own judgment, rather than depending on specific instructions for every situation.

3. **Building Problem-Solving Workshops**:

Companies can organize problem-solving workshops alongside formal training programs to tackle real business challenges. These workshops prompt employees to think critically and devise practical solutions, emphasizing the significance of simplicity and common sense in decision-making. They also foster cross-functional collaboration by encouraging employees from various departments to share their viewpoints and develop comprehensive, practical solutions.

Example: A great illustration of a common sense-based approach to issue solving is seen in Toyota's Kaizen workshops. Workers at all levels are encouraged to make suggestions for improving workflows; these suggestions typically center on small, gradual adjustments that boost productivity and cut down on waste. These courses use practical, hands-on decision-making to help build a culture of continuous improvement.

Rewarding Common-Sense Decisions: Incentivizing Practicality

In order to genuinely instill common sense in the corporate culture, employers must provide rewards to staff members who exhibit good judgment and useful problem-solving techniques. Businesses reaffirm that common sense and practicality are valued throughout the organization by praising and rewarding sensible judgments.

1. **Creating a Recognition Program for Practical Solutions**:

Encouraging common sense can be achieved by implementing a formal recognition program that showcases employees who devise uncomplicated and efficient solutions to business obstacles. These solutions may involve cost-saving measures, enhancements to processes, or innovations in customer service that exemplify common-sense reasoning. Acknowledging these endeavors publicly communicates to the entire organization that decisions based on common sense are highly regarded.

Example: Procter & Gamble (P&G) rewards staff members who devise workable solutions that lower expenses or enhance product quality. Through company-wide recognition programs, P&G rewards practical, real-world problem-solving, fostering a culture that values and encourages common sense thinking.

2. **Incentivizing Cost-Saving and Efficiency Improvements**:

Companies should also provide incentives to staff members who exhibit common sense thinking that results in cost savings or increases in operational efficiency. These incentives might take the form of cash payouts, bonuses, or promotions. Employees are encouraged to prioritize clarity and simplicity in their work as a result of the direct connection this establishes between practical decision-making and material rewards.

Example: During Jack Welch's leadership, General Electric (GE) placed a high priority on rewarding staff members who discovered ways to save expenses and increase productivity. Despite being extremely organized, the company's Six Sigma approach encouraged pragmatic thinking that resulted in reduced costs and more efficient operations. Workers who solved problems with this kind of common sense were given promotions and bonuses.

3. **Tying Common-Sense Thinking to Career Advancement**:

Career advancement in many firms is dependent on performance indicators such as customer happiness, project delivery, or sales performance. Companies that wish to foster a common sense culture should, however, also link professional advancement to staff members' capacity for critical thought, problem-solving efficiency, and the ability to simplify difficult situations. Businesses may guarantee that common-sense decision-making is transmitted up through the leadership ranks by establishing it as a prerequisite for advancement.

Example: Unilever places a strong emphasis on decision-making and practical problem-solving within its leadership development programs. Leaders are evaluated based on their capacity to achieve business objectives and their adeptness in applying common sense and judgment to attain those objectives. This method guarantees that practical thinking is deeply integrated into the company's leadership succession plan.

Fostering a Collaborative, Open Environment

Incorporating common sense into the business culture involves fostering an atmosphere that values candid feedback, teamwork, and communication. Workers ought to be at ease voicing their opinions, voicing problems, and proposing changes. Common sense reasoning is encouraged in a collaborative setting because it facilitates the open exchange of different viewpoints and approaches to issue solving.

1. **Encouraging Open Dialogue and Feedback**:

When staff members see inefficiencies, unduly complex procedures, or areas for improvement, they should feel free to voice their concerns. Leaders should encourage this kind of environment. Open communication empowers staff members to use common sense to recognize and resolve issues rather than mindlessly adhering to antiquated protocols.

Example: Employees at Google are encouraged to challenge ideas and provide feedback because of the company's open dialogue culture. Employee thoughts and suggestions are heard at regular meetings and forums, which fosters a culture of continual improvement based on sensible, real-world reasoning.

2. **Promoting Cross-Department Collaboration**:

Working across departments can sometimes yield the best workable answers to business issues. When workers from several departments collaborate, they can pool their knowledge to identify common sense solutions that are frequently overlooked in silos. This kind of cooperation pushes the organization as a whole to apply practical thinking more broadly.

Example: Cross-departmental collaboration is ingrained in the organizational culture of multinational design firm IDEO. Teams from a variety of fields, including engineering, business strategy, and design, collaborate to find solutions to challenging issues for their clients. This cooperative method produces inventive, useful solutions that meet demands in the actual world.

Building a Lasting Culture of Common Sense

In order for organizations to genuinely instill common sense in the corporate culture, they need not only promote practical thinking but also actively recruit, develop, and compensate staff members who exhibit these traits. Through the cultivation of a culture that prioritizes empowerment, transparency, simplicity, and teamwork, businesses can establish a conducive atmosphere for rational decision-making.

A business that effectively integrates common sense into its culture will experience improvements in problem-solving skills, employee engagement, agility, and long-term sustainability. In the end, cultivating a common sense culture makes sure that companies are better able to handle complexity, adjust to change, and produce steady, significant success.

Chapter 7: Common Sense in Innovation

A common attribute of successful businesses is innovation, which propels them into new product and service categories and markets. But in their haste to innovate, companies sometimes overlook common sense and pragmatism. This chapter looks at how creativity and disruption can coexist with practical application, sustainability, and commercial objectives by combining common sense and innovation. Companies should use common sense principles to make sure that their innovations are grounded in reality, in line with their primary objective, and able to provide long-term value, as opposed to pursuing innovation for its own sake.

Innovating Without Losing Sight of Basics

The desire for organizations to follow every new trend or technological advancement, even if it doesn't fit with their primary goals, is one of the biggest obstacles to innovation in business. While innovation is important, it must always be based in reality and in line with the company's overarching strategy and objectives, according to common sense. Common-sense innovation focuses on producing solutions that solve genuine problems for customers, improve operations, or create long-term value for the organization.

1. **Staying Focused on the Core Mission**:

Innovation shouldn't deviate too much from the main goals and advantages of the business. Common sense informs us that the best innovations are those that enhance or complement what a firm currently performs well. Businesses run the danger of squandering money and weakening their brand identity when they pursue innovations that are unrelated to their main business.

Example: Apple's approach to innovation is a prime illustration of practical wisdom. Despite its reputation for producing cutting-edge goods, Apple has always kept its inventions very close to its fundamental goal of making devices that are both aesthetically pleasing and easy to use. Rather than venturing into unrelated industries or trends, Apple's inventions, whether they be in the form of the iPhone, iPad, or MacBook, have constantly focused on improving the user experience.

2. **Avoiding "Shiny Object Syndrome"**:

Many businesses become focused on pursuing the newest trends or technologies without comprehensively grasping how these advancements will enhance their operations or serve their customers. This phenomenon is referred to as "shiny object syndrome", wherein companies allocate resources to new tools, technologies, or strategies solely because they are novel, rather than because they fulfill a distinct purpose. It is logical to conclude that innovation should address particular issues, rather than simply adhering to trends to project a modern image.

Example: The practicality of Google Glass was overshadowed by its innovation. Despite the excitement surrounding wearable technology and augmented reality, Google Glass didn't address a specific consumer need and its purpose was unclear. While the product was groundbreaking, it didn't offer practical benefits for regular users. A sensible strategy would have been to test the technology in smaller, more specific scenarios before a widespread release.

3. **Balancing Creativity with Feasibility**:

Innovation relies heavily on imagination, but it also needs to be tempered with practicality and viability. Businesses should use common sense when determining if an innovative idea can be implemented realistically given the existing resources and experience. Coming up with original ideas is not enough; those concepts also need to be workable, scalable, and in line with the objectives of the business.

Example: A fantastic example of striking a balance between innovation and practicality is Dyson's development of the bagless vacuum cleaner. James Dyson wanted to make a disposable bag-free vacuum that was easy for customers to use and didn't harm the environment. But Dyson made sure the vacuum's technology was functional, affordable, and scalable in order to strike a balance between creativity and reality. His sensible strategy produced a ground-breaking product that was well-received by consumers.

Lessons from Startups: Innovation with Practicality

Startups are often more agile, flexible, and open to taking risks than larger, established companies. However, the key factor that distinguishes successful startups from unsuccessful ones is their capacity to innovate in a manner that is both imaginative and pragmatic. The most successful startups employ practicality in their innovation approaches by remaining committed to addressing particular customer issues, swiftly adjusting to feedback, and making efficient use of limited resources.

1. **Customer-Centric Innovation**:

Successful startups frequently concentrate on providing workable, creative solutions to address actual client problem areas. They are motivated by a thorough comprehension of the demands of their clients and design their solutions to best address those needs. It is common sense to believe that the most innovative ideas originate from client feedback and are solutions that offer measurable, observable benefits.

Example: Airbnb initially began as a straightforward way to assist individuals in locating short-term accommodation by leasing out extra rooms or residences. The creators did not intend to establish a revolutionary technology company; they simply recognized a specific customer demand (inexpensive, short-term lodging) and utilized a logical method to address it. Consequently, Airbnb's platform expanded into a worldwide recognized brand by effectively addressing a genuine problem in a convenient, user-friendly manner.

2. **Iterative Innovation and Rapid Testing**:

Iterative innovation is a common strategy used by startups to test concepts fast, get customer feedback, and improve their goods and services. They can innovate while lowering risk and making sure they are satisfying customer needs thanks to this sensible strategy. Startups use lean approaches to test their innovations in tiny, manageable ways, as opposed to massively investing in a single, unproven idea.

Example: A basic MVP (minimum viable product) that let customers store and share files was what Dropbox started off as. Instead of spending years developing the complete product, the creators tested a preliminary version with consumers, collected feedback, and made ongoing platform improvements. Because to its sensible, iterative growth strategy, Dropbox was able to expand gradually without overspending on unproven concepts.

3. **Resource Efficiency and Scalability**:

Limited resources are a common challenge for startups, requiring them to be efficient in their innovations. It is important for startups to have a practical understanding of what can be achieved with their available resources and to gradually scale their operations. Startups that prioritize scalability from the beginning are more likely to achieve sustainable growth.

Example: Originally designed as a communication tool for a small team, Slack was later expanded to cater to external users. Slack's incremental development allowed for innovation without excessive spending on infrastructure or marketing, enabling the business to grow organically through practical means.

Avoiding the Hype Cycle: Staying Grounded Amidst Disruption

The business world experiences a repetitive cycle known as the hype cycle, in which new technologies or trends are enthusiastically introduced but eventually diminish as their limitations or impracticalities are revealed. While some disruptions endure and provide lasting value, many short-lived trends leave businesses that pursued them struggling to regain stability. It is advisable for businesses to stay pragmatic and assess whether new trends genuinely support their long-term objectives before committing time and resources.

1. **Evaluating New Trends with a Critical Eye**:

Leaders must evaluate new trends with a critical and objective mindset, questioning whether the technology or trend genuinely addresses customer needs and enhances operational efficiency. It is essential for leaders to conduct thorough research and testing of new trends before wholeheartedly embracing them, instead of hastily joining the trend.

Example: In fields where blockchain technology offered no discernible benefits, several businesses hurried to implement it. Even if supply chain management and finance are two areas where blockchain is most useful, many other industries adopted it only because it was a hot technology at the time. Walmart, on the other hand, used blockchain in a sensible manner, focusing on enhancing food safety through supply chain tracking of goods. Walmart avoided the hype by concentrating on a useful use and applied the technology to address an actual issue.

2. **Aligning Innovation with Long-Term Strategy**:

Companies should make sure that the innovations they implement support their long-term strategic objectives. It is common sense to realize that even the most innovative technology or trend will only be beneficial if it aids in the accomplishment of the company's primary goal. Businesses may guarantee the long-term, sustainable value of their investments in new technology or products by concentrating on innovations that complement their overall strategy.

Example: Tesla's innovations—which include energy storage, solar power, and electric cars—align with a long-term vision of a sustainable future. Every innovation made by Tesla, including its Powerwall batteries and electric cars, is in line with the company's goal of hastening the global switch to sustainable energy. Innovations from Tesla are based on a useful objective that directs the company's long-term growth, not only about upending sectors.

3. **Avoiding Innovation for the Sake of Innovation**:

Sometimes businesses make the mistake of innovating only to look cutting edge or to stay up with rivals. Common sense pushes innovators to have a clear goal in mind, making sure that every new concept fulfills a functional requirement and advances the success of the business. Purposeless innovation can result in unnecessary expenditure and lost possibilities to concentrate on more useful advancements.

Example: Quibi, a short-form video streaming service, exemplifies innovation without a clear purpose. Despite attempting to revolutionize content consumption, Quibi failed to cater to a specific customer demand and couldn't rival established platforms such as Netflix and YouTube. A more sensible approach would have entailed thorough market research and practical assessment of whether there was genuine consumer interest in a mobile-only, short-form streaming platform.

Common Sense Innovation in Established Companies

Big, well-established businesses have particular difficulties when it comes to innovation. Even though they have the financial means to engage in disruptive technologies and research and development, bureaucracy, risk aversion, and a lack of flexibility can hinder them. In well-established businesses, sensible innovation necessitates striking a balance between utilizing resources to propel expansion and making sure that new ideas stay narrowly focused, realistic, and in line with the organization's key goals.

1. **Encouraging Intrapreneurship**:

Encouraging intrapreneurship is a common-sense approach to fostering innovation within large companies, as it involves motivating employees at all levels to think and act like entrepreneurs. This enables companies to harness the creative potential of their workforce and ensures that new ideas are rooted in the company's real-world challenges and opportunities.

Example: With a long tradition of encouraging intrapreneurship, 3M allows its staff members to concentrate on side projects that result in useful inventions. Among the most well-known instances is the invention of Post-it Notes, a product that was needed but had not yet been developed by 3M workers. By taking a sensible approach to innovation, 3M is able to keep an eye on the needs of its customers and enhance its product line over time.

2. **Creating Innovation Labs for Practical Testing**:

By establishing innovation labs where new ideas are tested in small batches before being implemented across the entire firm, established businesses can apply common sense concepts to innovation. Through these labs, businesses can test new technologies and procedures without having to overinvest in resources or interfere with their regular business operations.

Example: Walmart's innovation hub, Walmart Labs, is where the business explores emerging technologies in a controlled setting, including blockchain, AI, and machine learning. With this strategy, Walmart may investigate novel ideas while using common sense to assess if these technologies would yield real benefits prior to putting them into widespread use.

3. **Scaling Innovation with Practicality in Mind**:

After a successful innovation, it is important for an established company to scale it carefully and sustainably. Scaling too rapidly without ensuring that processes, resources, and infrastructure are in place can result in operational difficulties. Common-sense innovation means scaling at a rate that the organization can manage while upholding quality and efficiency.

Example: IKEA's global business growth has been facilitated by its unwavering commitment to pragmatism. IKEA has made scalable and useful inventions, such flat-pack furniture and its in-store consumer experience. The business has grown steadily, making sure that every new market it enters is equipped to support its distinct business strategy. IKEA's common-sense approach to growing has allowed it to develop while retaining operational efficiency and customer happiness.

Building a Future of Practical Innovation

In a world where businesses are always being pushed to innovate, using common sense is essential to making sure that innovation stays useful, customer-focused, and long-lasting. Businesses should utilize common sense to anchor their innovation strategy in real-world difficulties, consumer demands, and long-term goals, rather than chasing trends or disrupting for the sake of disruption.

Businesses can produce innovations that not only draw notice but also provide long-term value by fusing creativity and pragmatism. Common sense assures that innovation is not simply about being the first to market with a new idea—it's about solving issues, improving lives, and building a future that is both innovative and founded in reality.

Chapter 8: The Future of Common Sense in Business

Looking forward to the fast-changing business environment, it's important to remember that common sense will remain a crucial principle for organizations dealing with change, unpredictability, and complexity. In this section, we will examine how common sense can act as a guiding factor in the future of business, especially in the realms of technology, leadership, and education. Whether it's the emergence of artificial intelligence and automation or the changing dynamics of the global workforce, companies that integrate common sense into their decision-making and strategies will be better prepared to adjust and succeed in the long run.

The Role of AI and Automation: Complementing, Not Replacing, Common Sense

Automation and artificial intelligence (AI) are changing industries and redefining what work will look like in the future. With the help of these technologies, decision-making based on data should be more productive and efficient. But even in the era of sentient robots, common sense is still indispensable. Artificial intelligence (AI) and automation both have their advantages in terms of process optimization and important insights, but they fall short of human intuition, experience, and judgment when it comes to making business decisions.

1. **AI as a Tool, Not a Replacement for Human Judgment**:

No matter how sophisticated the technology is, it is only as useful as the people who use it, as common sense tells us. While AI is capable of processing enormous volumes of data and spotting patterns, it is not equipped to make judgments that are human-centered or contextual. Instead of taking the role of human intuition, artificial intelligence (AI) should be viewed as an additional tool. Common sense will always be essential in difficult situations where many factors need to be considered, such moral quandaries, customer relationships, or erratic market fluctuations.

Example: AI in healthcare can evaluate patient data and provide recommendations for possible diagnosis, but doctors still have the last say in matters of medical judgment and common sense. Effective treatment requires human intuition, experience, and comprehension of each patient's unique situation.

2. **Balancing Data with Intuition in AI-Driven Decision Making**:

As businesses integrate AI more deeply into their operations, it's crucial for leaders to find a balance between data-driven insights and their own intuition and experience. AI can provide extremely detailed analytics, but it doesn't take into consideration the subtleties of human behavior, market sentiment, or real-time fluctuations. It's important for leaders to use their common sense and interpret data within the larger context, ensuring that AI-driven decisions don't overshadow their human understanding of the situation.

Example: Trading algorithms driven by AI in the financial services industry make choices based on market data. However, when there are unanticipated geopolitical developments, regulatory changes, or other human considerations that computers can't completely grasp, traders and portfolio managers frequently utilize their common sense to overturn algorithmic recommendations.

3. **Addressing Ethical Challenges in AI**:

The ethical dilemmas posed by the advancement of AI include worries about algorithmic bias and issues regarding the protection of data. It is crucial to employ common sense in addressing these dilemmas, as it serves as a guiding principle for organizations to make decisions that are not only in line with the law but also morally upright. Companies need to exercise common sense to guarantee the responsible use of AI technologies and their positive impact on society, rather than solely focusing on financial gains.

Example: Microsoft prioritizes accountability, openness, and fairness in its AI principles. The business has put in place internal review procedures to make sure that its AI systems adhere to moral principles, using common sense to take into account the potential social effects of emerging technologies. This strategy has established a standard that other IT businesses may adhere to when using AI responsibly.

Educating the Next Generation of Leaders: Reintroducing Common Sense in Business Education

The upcoming generation of leaders will need to possess not only technical understanding but also the common sense and practical judgment needed to make wise judgments in unpredictable circumstances, as firms encounter more complex difficulties. However, theoretical models, analytics, and data-driven decision-making are frequently overemphasized in contemporary management education. In order to equip future leaders, it is imperative that business schools incorporate common sense back into their curricula.

1. **Balancing Theory with Practical Application**:

Traditional business schools focus primarily on intricate theories, financial models, and abstract ideas. Despite their significance, these concepts are frequently detached from the practical aspects of daily business activities. It is widely understood that practical experience and hands-on problem-solving skills are equally essential for achieving success as academic theory. Therefore, business education must find a middle ground between theoretical understanding and real-world implementation.

Example: Babson College incorporates real-world business initiatives into its curriculum to give students real-world experience in addition to its entrepreneurship focus. With the help of this practical method, students may apply common sense reasoning to real-world issues, preparing them for leadership positions that require them to make snap decisions.

2. **Teaching Critical Thinking and Judgment**:

The capacity for critical thought and the ability to make decisions under unclear circumstances are closely linked to common sense. Business schools should emphasize on building these talents in future leaders, educating them to evaluate complicated events holistically and make judgments based on a mix of evidence, experience, and intuition. Case studies and role-playing activities that mimic making decisions in the real world should be incorporated into courses to help students develop their practical judgment.

Example: Through the use of case studies, the Harvard Business School encourages students to evaluate business problems from several perspectives and reach conclusions based on their judgment. This method mimics the complexity of the actual world and equips students to use common sense in addition to technical expertise to think critically in unforeseen circumstances.

3. **Incorporating Soft Skills and Emotional Intelligence into the Curriculum**:

The growing recognition by businesses of the importance of emotional intelligence (EQ) in leadership calls for business education to place equal emphasis on the development of soft skills like empathy, communication, and flexibility. Understanding people—whether they be stakeholders, customers, or employees—is frequently at the heart of common sense in leadership. Students who learn effective communication, conflict resolution, and relationship management skills will be better prepared to use common sense in leadership positions.

Example: The Stanford Graduate School of Business focuses on developing interpersonal dynamics and leadership skills through its courses, which aim to cultivate soft skills and equip students with the ability to lead with empathy and practical judgment. By prioritizing emotional intelligence, the school ensures that its graduates can effectively apply common-sense principles to navigate complex human challenges in the business world.

Building a Lasting Legacy with Common Sense

To stay competitive in the long term, businesses must establish a sustainable tradition of practical wisdom. This involves developing adaptable systems, processes, and cultures that prioritize delivering lasting value. Companies that consistently employ common sense will be more equipped to navigate economic fluctuations, industry changes, and shifting customer demands.

1. **Embedding Flexibility and Adaptability into the Organizational Culture**:

Because the future is unpredictable, companies must have the adaptability to adjust to shifting market conditions. Common-sense thinking supports agility—the capacity to turn rapidly when necessary and to make judgments based on the present environment rather than being trapped into inflexible plans. Businesses that integrate flexibility into their culture will be more equipped to take advantage of opportunities and reduce risks in a world that is changing quickly.

Example: Netflix has a reputation for being flexible. When the chance presented itself, Netflix, which had previously offered DVD rentals, switched to streaming and then went on to produce original content. The business kept its sensible focus on providing value to customers during these changes, adjusting to new technologies and viewing preferences without losing sight of its basic objective.

2. **Long-Term Thinking and Sustainability**:

In today's consumer landscape, the emphasis on environmental and social responsibility is growing, requiring businesses to prioritize sustainable, long-range approaches. It is logical for companies to avoid prioritizing short-term profits over long-term benefits. Rather, they should allocate resources to sustainable initiatives that safeguard the environment, contribute to their communities, and guarantee the endurance of their business operations.

Example: The Unilever Sustainable Living Plan is a long-term sustainability strategy that Unilever executed under Paul Polman's direction. This common sense strategy increased the company's profitability while lowering its negative effects on the environment, promoting health and well-being, and improving livelihoods. Unilever created an enduring legacy that was in line with changing customer expectations by striking a balance between short-term business needs and long-term sustainability.

3. **Fostering Innovation Through Common-Sense Leadership**:

Business success will still be propelled by innovation, but companies that base their innovation strategies on practicality will gain a competitive advantage. Instead of pursuing innovation just for the sake of it, leaders need to guarantee that new ideas are feasible, scalable, and in line with the company's overall mission. Common-sense innovation involves striking a balance between creativity and practicality, making sure that every new product or service delivers tangible value for the business and its customers.

Example: The focus of Tesla's advancements in electric vehicles and renewable energy extends beyond technological progress; it revolves around the practical objective of lessening carbon emissions and shifting the world towards sustainable energy. Tesla's executives have upheld a pragmatic strategy towards innovation, guaranteeing that their products are not only pioneering but also adaptable to fulfill worldwide needs.

Common Sense as a Competitive Advantage

Businesses who can apply common sense will increasingly have an advantage over their competitors as the business environment grows more complex and technology advances. The most successful businesses will be distinguished from those that battle with overcomplication and inefficiency by their capacity to simplify difficult issues, make prompt and sensible decisions, and concentrate on long-term sustainability.

1. **Keeping Decision-Making Simple and Efficient**:

Leaders can simplify decision-making by using common sense, which helps them cut through bureaucracy and avoid unnecessary complexity. Companies that can quickly make clear decisions in response to market changes will be more agile and better positioned to take advantage of new opportunities. In the future, businesses that are able to think clearly and act decisively will distinguish themselves.

Example: Toyota Production System (TPS) is Toyota's lean manufacturing system, which focuses on simplicity, efficiency, and continuous improvement. Toyota has established a durable competitive advantage in operational efficiency and product quality by implementing common sense in its production processes.

2. **Focusing on People in a Technology-Driven World**:

Despite the increasing reliance of businesses on technology, basic sense tells us that people are the foundation of every firm. Businesses that make investments in their workforce, cultivate enduring relationships with clients, and establish a healthy work atmosphere will maintain a competitive edge over time. Empowering staff members to create and solve problems is the main goal of common-sense leadership, which also makes sure that technology enhances rather than supplants human innovation.

Example: Southwest Airlines is known for its high customer satisfaction ratings, mainly due to its emphasis on people, including both employees and passengers. The company's leadership encourages employees to take actions that prioritize the needs of customers, and this practical approach to customer service has resulted in long-term loyalty.

The Future Belongs to Common-Sense Thinkers

In the ever-changing business landscape, companies that integrate practical wisdom into their strategy will thrive. Whether it's adapting to the emergence of AI, preparing the next generation of leaders, or establishing a lasting legacy, common-sense principles will be essential for navigating the complexities and uncertainties ahead. By staying rooted in practicality, prioritizing long-term value, and maintaining a people-centric approach, companies can ensure not only competitiveness but also resilience in the face of change.

Common sense is more than just a business tactic; it's a mindset that can revolutionize organizations, empower individuals, and fuel progress. In a future marked by swift technological progress and global upheavals, common sense will continue to be the cornerstone of building sustainable, adaptable, and successful enterprises.

Conclusion: A Call to Action

As we come to the end of this investigation, it is evident that common sense is not just essential but also increasingly scarce in today's business environment. We are living in an era where complexity is highly valued, and decisions are often obscured by layers of data, technical language, and intricate procedures. However, amidst all the chaos, common sense remains one of the most potent tools available to business leaders, entrepreneurs, and professionals. This section serves as a call to action—an urging to reintroduce common sense into the core of decision-making, strategy, and daily activities. It serves as a reminder that simplicity, practicality, and wise judgment are not just relics of the past but rather the keys to unlocking a more effective and prosperous future.

A Call to Action: Reintroducing Common Sense in Business

In positions of leadership, whether in a large corporation, a small business, or in one's career, it is important to base decisions on common sense principles. Throughout this book, we have observed how the effective application of common sense can simplify processes, boost employee efficiency, strengthen customer connections, and promote lasting growth. However, it takes deliberate action and hard work to reintegrate these principles into environments that have become overwhelmed by complexity.

1. **Leaders Must Lead by Example**:

A key factor in restoring common sense to business is leadership. Leaders set the tone for their organizations, and they can encourage their colleagues to follow suit by modeling sensible communication, decision-making, and problem-solving techniques. Simplifying techniques, acting swiftly when the answers are obvious, and allowing staff members to exercise independent judgment are the first steps toward achieving this.

Call to Action for Leaders: Are the procedures within your company needlessly complicated? Do you cultivate an atmosphere where staff members are encouraged to take charge? Actively work on streamlining and having faith in your team's real-world decision-making ability. Eliminate redundant authorization levels and concentrate on distinct, achievable objectives that everyone can grasp and contribute to.

2. **Entrepreneurs Should Focus on What Matters**:

Entrepreneurs often feel the urge to follow every trend, try out every new technology, or introduce overly complicated solutions. However, achieving success frequently involves maintaining simplicity and concentrating on the fundamental aspects of the business. It's evident that addressing genuine customer needs and operating efficiently are the key factors for long-term growth.

Call to Action for Entrepreneurs: Consider your business model carefully. Are you pursuing complexity just for the sake of innovation, or are you providing genuine value to your customers in the most straightforward and efficient manner? Use practical judgment to improve your products, simplify operations, and make sure that every choice supports your company's long-term objectives and principles.

3. **Professionals Should Trust Their Instincts**:

In today's data-driven world, professionals are often trained to depend only on metrics and intricate systems, but it's essential to remember that intuition, experience, and practical judgment are just as crucial. It's important for professionals to find a balance between their expertise and their gut feelings to make decisions that are practical and realistic.

Call to Action for Professionals: Avoid letting overthinking or your fear of making mistakes get in the way of your progress. Especially when your experience tells you that an easy-to-solve answer is in front of you, trust your gut. Whether you're managing your workload, working with coworkers, or resolving customer issues, use common sense to inform your decisions.

Common Sense Is the Competitive Advantage

In a society where decision-making is often dominated by complexity and overanalysis, common sense serves as a valuable distinguishing factor. It effectively navigates through the confusion, providing clarity and effectiveness. Companies that adopt common sense as a guiding value can achieve a considerable competitive edge, allowing them to be more flexible, more creative, and more responsive to the requirements of their customers and employees.

1. **Simplicity Drives Agility**:

Future-proof firms are ones that can quickly adjust to changing conditions. With its emphasis on practical solutions and simplicity, common sense helps companies be flexible and respond to changes without becoming bogged down in layers of red tape or pointless procedures. By streamlining operations, organizations can make faster, more effective decisions—giving them a competitive edge in an ever-evolving market.

Example: Simplifying their operations has been the cornerstone of success for businesses such as IKEA and Southwest Airlines. By concentrating on simple, effective business models, they have been able to lower expenses, adjust to changes in the industry, and provide clients with continuous value. Their common-sense approach helps them to move faster than competitors who are weighed down by complexity.

2. **Customer Focus Through Practicality**:

Many businesses forget the fundamentals of solving client problems in the most efficient and practical way possible in this day of rapid innovation. Simpleness is valued by clients, as common sense informs us. They seek out goods and services that are user-friendly, dependable, and considerate to their needs. In a congested market, companies that prioritize useful innovations and customer-focused solutions will stand out.

Example: Apple's ability to make complicated technology simple is the key to its success. The company has one of the most devoted customer bases in the world thanks to its emphasis on the user experience and creation of intuitive, user-friendly products. One important factor that keeps Apple ahead of rivals who frequently overcomplicate their products is its commonsense approach to design.

3. **Efficiency and Cost-Effectiveness**:

Cost-effective operations are also the result of common sense. Organizations may maximize their resources, cut down on waste, and function more efficiently by getting rid of superfluous complexity and concentrating on what matters most. This raises profitability and puts the business in a stronger position during lean economic times.

Example: The success of common sense is demonstrated by Toyota's lean manufacturing system. Toyota has remained one of the top automakers in the world by emphasizing productivity, cutting waste, and ongoing improvement. Its sensible production methods have provided it with a sustainable cost and quality competitive advantage.

4. **Building Long-Term Sustainability**:

Lastly, firms can build long-term viability on the foundation of common sense. Common-sense businesses concentrate on generating value that endures rather than pursuing quick profits. This entails making choices that put the environment, the company's long-term health, and its workers first. By avoiding the traps of short-term thinking, common sense helps firms stay competitive for years to come.

Example: Unilever's dedication to sustainability is based on rational reasoning. Rather than simply maximizing short-term profits, Unilever has focused on building a business model that supports long-term environmental and social goals. This strategy has guaranteed the company's long-term survival in a world where sustainability is becoming more and more important, while also fortifying its brand and drawing in devoted clients.

The Enduring Power of Common Sense

As this book has shown, common sense is not a thing of the past; rather, it is an enduring philosophy that provides organizations with a clear, purposeful, and focused approach to navigating complexity. In a world where complexity becomes more and more valued in and of itself, those who go back to making decisions based on experience and practicality will have an advantage.

Seeing the obvious when others are preoccupied with the complex is what it means to have common sense. It's about realizing that, on occasion, the simplest solution is the best one. It's about giving individuals the power to make decisions, concentrating on pressing issues, and applying reasonable judgment. Businesses can cut through the clutter, boost productivity, and promote long-term success when they adopt common sense.

Common sense is the competitive advantage that will make you stand out in a world that is changing quickly. It's time to reintroduce it into all facets of your company, including customer service, innovation, and leadership. Not only is common sense an effective instrument for success, but it is also essential to creating a future where companies prosper, people have agency, and clients are respected.

www.ingramcontent.com/pod-product-compliance
Lightning Source LLC
Chambersburg PA
CBHW050328230526
45471CB00005B/2396